2020-2021

# A Guide to First-Year Writing at GRAND VALLEY STATE UNIVERSITY

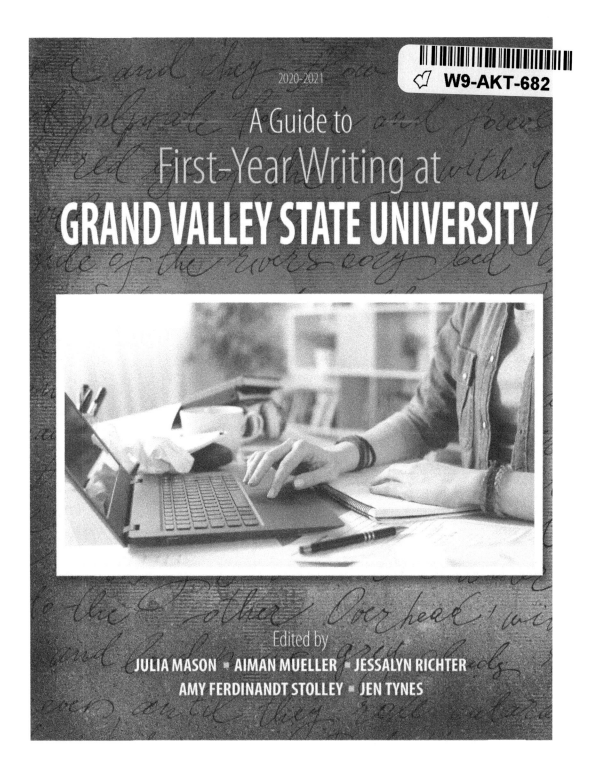

Edited by

**JULIA MASON** ▪ **AIMAN MUELLER** ▪ **JESSALYN RICHTER**
**AMY FERDINANDT STOLLEY** ▪ **JEN TYNES**

**Kendall Hunt**
publishing company

Cover Image © 2020 by GRAND VALLEY STATE UNIVERSITY.
Reprinted by permission.

www.kendallhunt.com
*Send all inquiries to*:
4050 Westmark Drive
Dubuque, IA 52004-1840

# CONTENTS

# INTRODUCTION

The first-year writing courses offered by the Department of Writing at Grand Valley State University are designed to build on and expand your writing, critical thinking, collaboration, and information literacy skills. This book, *A Guide to First-Year Writing at Grand Valley State University,* is meant to do just that—*guide* you in this class. (From here on, we will just call this book the *Guide.*) As a community of writers, we have worked to create a resource that invites you into our community and celebrates student writing at all stages. We hope you will make extensive use of the *Guide,* both in class and on your own, to succeed in first-year writing at Grand Valley.

Our Department of Writing strives to create a consistent program for all students who take first-year writing classes. Our professors teach using their own preferred teaching methods, but important elements remain consistent across all sections, such as learning outcomes, grading criteria, grading methods, and departmental policies, all of which you will find explained in this book. Each semester every first-year writing instructor meets once a week with other instructors to discuss these course goals and expectations as they apply to particular students' papers. At the end of the term, these groups of instructors read final portfolios of the work that students produce and assign each portfolio a grade. As a result, at Grand Valley, you can compare your grade at the end of your first-year writing experience fairly with the grade of every other student on campus who has taken first-year writing here.

This Guide tells you more about our shared course expectations for first-year writing at Grand Valley. To start, we provide brief descriptions of the different courses you can choose to complete your General Education Foundations—Writing requirement, just in case you wish to reconsider your choice of the right place to start your college writing experience. Then we provide a much more detailed overview of the first-year writing courses we offer so you know the goals we have set out for your learning. Next, we explore the key principles of how and why we write in college that will shape the work you do in class, which is followed by the University and Writing Department policies that apply to this course. The next section focuses on the first-year writing portfolio, where we outline our grading policies, submission guidelines, and responses to questions many students enrolled in the course ask. We then provide resources that are available for all student writers at Grand Valley, but that are particularly useful for students enrolled in first-year writing courses. Finally, you'll find examples of writing completed last year that earned As, including entire portfolios and some single standout essays. You will use these samples of student writing to guide your revisions and spur classroom discussion of the grading expectations.

You'll also find some advice from students who have taken first-year writing classes in the past. You'll see quotes from Professor Aiman Mueller's students throughout the first part of the book, and along with the exemplary student writing you'll read, you'll hear about the writers' experiences in writing classes and advice for you as you start this semester. We share these students' experiences with you here because we think hearing from former writing students will be helpful, though we're sure you'll come up with your own words of wisdom to share at the end of the semester too.

## FIRST-YEAR WRITING COURSE OPTIONS

As you know by now, you decide which writing course you should take first at Grand Valley after considering information about our departmental requirements and consulting with advisors during orientation. You have these two choices:

▶ WRT 150 is for students who are prepared to meet the goals of the general education (GE) writing requirement in **one semester**. These students write fluently and are ready to begin college-level academic writing, including writing with sources.

▶ WRT 120 and 130 (Stretch) are for students who prefer to spend **two semesters** building the skills required by GE writing requirement. Students have more time to practice skills and meet the goals of the first-year writing requirement.

Just in case you would like to consider your choice one more time, here are brief descriptions of your other options. If you have doubts about the course you have chosen, talk about your concerns with your professor as soon as possible. Your professor may also assign a quick writing task during the first week of the course, in part to help you make that decision.

## WRT 120 and 130 (Stretch)

This two-sequence course gives students additional time and support to develop the skills required by the first-year writing curriculum. Students will meet the same outcomes as students who take WRT 150 and will complete assignments similar to those in 150 but will do so in two semesters instead of one. By working with the same instructor all year, students will receive more support toward reaching their writing goals.

## WRT 150

Writing 150 is the standard option for students seeking to fulfill the General Education first-year writing requirement. This class focuses on academic writing, with a special emphasis on research-based writing, and assumes some prior experience with academic writing and computers.

# OVERVIEW OF FIRST-YEAR WRITING

Because all students are required to complete a first-year writing course at Grand Valley to prepare you for the writing you will do as a student here, our courses focus on academic writing, including writing informed by scholarly research. Instructors assume that as a student in WRT 130 or WRT 150, you are ready to read, summarize, and analyze a wide variety of college-level published material. In most WRT 150 classes, you first write four or five papers. In WRT 130 classes, you will write one to two new essays and continue revising the work you began in WRT 120. In both WRT 150 and WRT 130, at least one of your essays (but likely more) will integrate material from highly credible sources that you will find through extensive academic research. You should expect that most of these papers will be four to eight pages long in normal academic format. From among these papers, you will pick three, including at least one that demonstrates your ability to find and integrate source material effectively, to include in your final portfolio for grading. Then, you will spend a considerable amount of time revising and improving your three portfolio papers.

In first-year writing classes, you will encounter challenging reading material—whether you find it in assigned readings or in your own research materials—and you will practice discussing, summarizing, and analyzing that material. You will also work on improving your writing processes so you can complete new kinds of writing tasks and rise to new levels of writing ability—processes that move effectively from prewriting, inventing, planning, and drafting to revising, consulting, editing, and finishing.

In most sections, you will meet in a computer classroom one day a week. Each computer is connected to the Internet and the Grand Valley network. The Grand Valley network includes personal storage space on the campus server and special access to research sources maintained by Grand Valley's library system. First-year writing instructors assume that you have a basic familiarity with computers, word processors, Web browsers, and e-mail.

After you have completed your General Education Foundations—Writing requirement through WRT 150 or WRT 120 and 130, you will be a more experienced college writer who will be able to:

### Prewrite, Invent, and Plan

▶ Read and understand material written for college audiences.

▶ Develop clearly focused written summaries, analyses, and paraphrases that demonstrate an understanding of the material you have read.

▶ Develop ideas using a variety of prewriting techniques, which may include brainstorming, freewriting, journal-keeping, consulting with others, conducting library research, and analyzing your audiences.

### Revise, Develop, and Shape

▶ Develop writing from early, writer-oriented drafts to later, reader-oriented drafts.

▶ Produce effective writing for a variety of purposes, such as narrating, explaining, exploring, and persuading.

▶ Demonstrate the ability to focus your writing on supportable themes, claims, or theories.

▶ Support your focus using well-selected details that are accurate and relevant.

▶ Consult with peer reviewers and other readers to assess the further needs of your drafts.

▶ Revise writing with particular audiences in mind, including academic audiences.

▶ Conduct effective, significant scholarly research.

▶ Integrate facts and opinions from a variety of sources into your own writing.

### *Refine, Edit, and Finish*

- ► Include words, facts, and ideas from research sources in ways that fully credit the original source and avoid plagiarism.
- ► Control the main features of a specific documentation style (like MLA or APA).
- ► Refine your sentence structures to produce an effective style and voice.
- ► Edit writing so that academic audiences can read the writing without having their attention and understanding diverted by problems in grammar, spelling, punctuation, and format.

In addition to requiring students to complete a first-year writing course, Grand Valley supports the development of your writing ability in other courses. Many General Education courses also focus on developing your writing in specific academic areas. After building that foundation, you will take two courses in disciplines of interest to you specifically designated as Supplemental Writing Skills courses. You may also take further writing courses, and many of your college courses will involve extensive writing. Thus, your first-year writing course is not the end of your college writing instruction. Instead, it seeks to supply you with an important foundation that you will build on for the rest of your college career.

> *"Do not be afraid of writing. Don't take so much time to plan how to make the perfect essay; just write and be willing to revise."*
>
> *—Brendan K.*

Finally, WRT 130 and WRT 150 are also part of your General Education Foundation coursework, and like all GE courses, we work to improve intellectual skills that you will use in later courses and in your life after college. In WRT 130 and WRT 150, we focus mainly on improving your skills in Written Communication, but we also strive to develop your Information Literacy skills. Throughout the semester, your instructor should assign and provide feedback on activities related to your ability to identify, evaluate, and work with different forms of information.

# FIRST-YEAR WRITING GOALS

By the end of WRT 130 or WRT 150, your final portfolio should demonstrate that you have achieved the program's goals and can perform each of these tasks:

## *Content and Development*

- ▶ Offer readers a clear purpose for reading.
- ▶ Maintain a single focus throughout the entire paper.
- ▶ Present ideas and descriptions that engage a college-level audience in your discussion.
- ▶ Conduct college-level research to find credible source material for a variety of purposes.
- ▶ Present a claim or focus that is developed with discussion, details, and examples, including graphics when useful.
- ▶ Discover and integrate sufficient material from outside sources to demonstrate your abilities in college-level writing, research, and thinking.

## *Organization*

- ▶ Establish an overall pattern for a paper to follow.
- ▶ Progress from one point, idea, or scene to another in a coherent, logical way.
- ▶ Construct paragraphs that are generally well-organized within the overall pattern of a paper.
- ▶ Lead readers through the order of your discussion in obvious and helpful ways.

## *Style*

- ▶ Craft sentences with purposefully chosen words and phrases.
- ▶ Structure sentences effectively to be clear, logical, and readable.
- ▶ Use a variety of sentence structures for good reasons.
- ▶ Maintain an overall voice in each paper that is appropriate for its purpose, genre, and audiences.

## *Mechanics*

- ▶ Adopt a format that is acceptable and appropriate for academic writing.
- ▶ Refer to outside sources that are introduced, integrated, and documented.
- ▶ Attend carefully to grammar, spelling, punctuation, and usage in final, edited writing.
- ▶ Use with care a standard academic style guide, such as the MLA or APA style guides.

# HOW AND WHY WE WRITE

## WRITING AS A PROCESS

When we think of writers, we might imagine people who possess some magical talent that allows them to sit down and instantly transfer their thoughts onto paper. But researchers have concluded that expert writers do not simply sit down and "put it in writing" in one easy step. Rather, successful experienced writers work through a complex process to get to their final product. Different writers follow different steps in that process depending on their needs and personal preferences, but in general, expert writers experience writing as a process that unfolds over time, not as a "one and done" burst of inspiration.

For instance, when faced with the need to communicate to an audience, experienced writers begin by exploring their own knowledge, feelings, and beliefs; considering the knowledge, feelings, and beliefs of their intended readers; and searching for something specific that needs to be said. Then they explore their communication options—the various forms available to them—before sketching out, reconsidering, revising, and polishing their message, making sure they are sensitive to their readers. Often, at several points during the writing process, expert writers ask friends or peers—people no more expert than they are, and often less so—to take a look at their drafted material and give advice or feedback. Finally, when satisfied with their efforts, expert writers polish the results and deliver their writing to their intended audience.

The example above illustrates five basic parts of a successful writing process:

- ▶ **Prewriting and Inventing**: generating ideas; forming questions for investigation and constructing a research plan; collecting, evaluating, and managing information from various sources; identifying possible subjects, purposes, audiences, and forms.
- ▶ **Planning and Drafting**: trying out ideas and approaches; zeroing in on a single focus and a single form.
- ▶ **Consulting**: talking with people about preliminary ideas, plans, and drafts; soliciting oral and written feedback from friends and colleagues about content, structure, audience appeal, style, and correctness.
- ▶ **Revising and Shaping**: considering additions and deletions; reshaping and refocusing existing material; and editing for style, flow, and obvious error.
- ▶ **Editing and Finishing**: taking authorial responsibility for the final product; editing carefully for correctness and format; and delivering the final product to its intended audience (instructor, relative, client, committee, editor, etc.).

Although the list above outlines the steps expert writers take as they complete writing projects, it is important to note that they don't always happen in order. There is no "correct" writing process. Some writers may follow the steps in order, but others might start with consulting, move on to drafting, and then work on invention activities to help generate new ideas or an organizational structure for the essay. Over the course of the semester, you'll find the process and strategies that work best for *you* as a writer, and you can apply those strategies to other writing tasks you'll encounter as a student and in the workplace.

## Developing Your Writing Process With New Strategies

While you will probably have a unique way of going through the steps set out above, at some point all expert writers need to find new ways of addressing the concerns of each step effectively. As instructors of first-year writing, we are not merely judges of your writing. In fact, you might best view instructors as coaches whose primary goal is to help you develop processes that you will use for the writing you do in this class, in future Grand Valley classes, and on the job. We help you explore your writing processes through class information, class discussions, stimulating writing assignments, and responses to your writing in progress.

Your instructor will help you explore your writing processes, but you can take control of your own processes by considering the following checklist that we have devised to help you develop expert methods. You don't need to do all of the strategies listed here, but we encourage you to try a few in each category and reflect on how it changes and improves your writing process.

> "Work on small amounts every day, whether it's just writing one paragraph, finding one source, or coming up with a single idea."
> —Philip B.

### Prewriting and Inventing

- ▶ Use a variety of brainstorming techniques to generate, develop, and focus topics.
- ▶ Write informally in journals or notebooks as an ongoing writer's activity.
- ▶ Use writing as a tool for learning as well as communicating.
- ▶ Analyze audience as a method of planning and focusing.
- ▶ Consider purpose, style, and form in relation to audience during the planning stages.
- ▶ Weigh a variety of form and style options during the planning stages.
- ▶ Sequence and initiate your own writing process to suit immediate purposes.
- ▶ Generate and select your own methods for developing material.
- ▶ Engage in prewriting discussions with your instructor and peers.
- ▶ Read as a writer; read published materials critically.
- ▶ Write and speak about yourself as a writer.
- ▶ Form questions for investigation and construct a research plan.
- ▶ Collect, evaluate, and manage information.
- ▶ Use basic reference materials (dictionary, encyclopedia, online search engine).

- ► Use research as a form of generating ideas and planning writing.
- ► Consider how numerical and graphic information or images might support your focus and purpose.

### Planning and Drafting

- ► Translate prewriting activities into drafts.
- ► Adapt your writing for specific readers, including academic ones.
- ► Write for broad, public, academic audiences.
- ► Vary diction and tone according to audience.
- ► Establish and maintain a focus that has a purpose.
- ► Maintain a consistent style throughout the different parts.
- ► Cultivate an appropriate and interesting voice.
- ► Integrate ideas and information from outside sources.
- ► Support ideas and observations with details, including numerical and graphic information and images.
- ► Save different drafts with different file names when you make important changes.

### Consulting

- ► Use feedback from peers.
- ► Give feedback to peers.
- ► Engage in revision discussions with your instructor, peers, and writing consultant.
- ► Survey and integrate readers' needs and interests.
- ► Write alternate and more fully realized new versions of earlier drafts.
- ► Work productively in writing groups.

### Revising and Shaping

- ► Write and use your own evaluations of your drafts.
- ► Adapt the style and voice of your language to suit your purpose and audience.
- ► Revise for focus, development, order, structure, balance, and emphasis.

- ► Align the information and reasoning in the paper with the paper's focus.
- ► Add, delete, change, or recast material to suit your purposes and readers.
- ► Establish a clear focus throughout the paper.
- ► Consider the wide variety of readers for whom you might actually be writing.
- ► Revise paragraphing and sentences for greater clarity and interest.
- ► Achieve "closure" in later drafts; make sure the product can become a consistent whole work.

### Editing and Finishing

- ► Proofread all writing intended for public audiences.
- ► Use your word processor's editing software to help you spot possible areas for improvement.
- ► Refresh your editing eye and ear by using methods like reading aloud, reading sentences in reverse order, reading as if you were somebody else (like your favorite uncle or aunt), or putting the latest draft away for a day or two.
- ► Use a dictionary and handbook for editing.
- ► Check your documentation with a guide for your documentation style.
- ► Check your use of material from sources to be sure you are using source material ethically.

## Responding to Peer Writing

Most instructors have students offer valuable feedback on each other's papers for two good reasons. Peer review will give you valuable feedback from peers to help you improve your drafts to help you think critically about your writing. You'll also get the chance to see how your classmates responded to the same assignment prompt you did, which can help generate ideas for how you might revise or refocus your own essay. We encourage students to practice peer review on their own, outside of class. As you practice peer review, you should avoid closing the door with final negative or positive evaluations on students' papers. If you judge early drafts

> *"Don't tell yourself that you can't write something. You may not think you're creative, but you are . . . Write as frequently as you can. Write and revise. Let others see your writing. Know how to use feedback. Let others know that you appreciate their feedback."*
>
> — *Tim H.*

by saying "your opening is perfect" or "this is already an A paper," you encourage your peers to stop rethinking and rewriting their papers. That might feel good for a moment, but it will not help anyone to improve.

Your instructor will probably have many suggestions about how to do successful peer reviews. Generally, experts in writing say to focus on global issues before moving on to local issues. Global revision means seeing the "big picture" and focusing on organization, and development of ideas, audience, and tone. Local revision means paying attention to details and focusing on editing for word choice, sentence fluency, grammar, spelling, and punctuation.

## INFORMATION LITERACY AND ACADEMIC CONVERSATIONS

As academic writers, we work in a world of information and opinion, so it is very common for us to refer to facts and ideas originally published in other sources, and then to quote and cite those sources in ways that carefully show where we got our information. Educators commonly refer to this skill as "information literacy," and it's a set of practices that is valued highly in universities across the country, including Grand Valley.

Information literacy is a crucial skill in your development as a writer because it offers you strategies for participating in academic conversations. That may sound like a strange phrase—academic conversations—and it might evoke images of tweed-wearing professors debating obscure points of philosophy. While that might still happen somewhere, most academic conversations today are conducted in the writing of academic papers. In writing studies, we often refer to academic writing as a conversation because a good writer is in *dialogue* with the sources he or she chooses to integrate into the essay. A writer might agree with a source and use it to verify the argument he is making, or a writer might disagree with a source but still use its ideas as a springboard for making her own argument. Either way, when writers engage with sources and incorporate them into their writing, they are participating in an ongoing conversation with other writers and thinkers engaged and interested in a specific issue, and they use their information literacy skills to do so.

We focus on information literacy in first-year writing classes for three main reasons. First, we want readers to take our writing seriously because we have done our homework, so to speak, by taking the time to find out what the credible authorities on the subject have already said. Second, we want our readers to understand how our own ideas relate to those of credible experts. Third, we want to give proper credit to those who have already written on the subject; after all, we want credit for our own work, so we must afford others the same courtesy. Together, these three goals help us to accomplish our larger goal of participating in ongoing scholarly and expert conversations—which is really what research writing does, at its best.

Doing that work well starts with doing excellent research—going beyond the world of mere opinions that are so easily available on the Internet and learning how to find, read, and use the kind of information on which experts rely.

Research is a key step in any writer's process, and it's one that can strongly influence the outcome of your final product. Grand Valley's expert research librarians have developed "Information Literacy Core Competencies" (ILCCs) for college students, defining six main goals for college-level research. According to the ILCCs, as a college-level researcher, you should learn to:

► construct a question or problem statement,
► locate and gather information,
► evaluate sources,
► manage information,
► use information ethically, and
► communicate knowledge.

You will develop these abilities throughout your college career, but WRT 130 or WRT 150 will give a strong foundation in all these areas. In your first-year writing class you will learn to *construct research questions* to develop a preliminary focus to help you manage the range of material that you might pursue. You will learn to *create a plan* for your search for information and identify the resources that will be available to help you (such as library guides, access to scholarly journals through online reference tools called databases, and the research librarians themselves). You will learn to *evaluate sources* so that you use the most appropriate and effective information rather than just the materials that pop up first in a Web search. You will learn to *manage information* in ways that help you keep track of what you have found and lower the stress and anxiety of conducting complicated research. Of course, as we reemphasize in many ways in this *Guide,* you will learn to *use information ethically* by giving other writers credit for what you have learned from them and for what they have written. By learning to cite sources correctly, you learn to avoid plagiarism, honor copyright, and participate expertly in academic discussions. Finally, we want you to *communicate knowledge* effectively by coming to understand how those academic discussions take place, and then by participating in those discussions.

We cannot overemphasize the importance of these information literacy competencies as part of an effective academic writing process. Information literacy does not always show up directly in grading criteria because it is essentially a process, not a product; yet information literacy will have a profound effect on your ability to communicate your ideas to an audience effectively.

## Sources and Evidence

When we talk about information literacy in first-year writing classes, we pay attention to the types of sources and types of evidence that students use to support their discussions about the topics they choose. In your previous writing classes, much of your research was probably done with Google—finding online sources that prove the point you want to make (or maybe help you figure out what you want your point to be). While those are certainly valid sources and can be part of the research you conduct in this class, your instructor will work with you to use library resources to find deeper and more complex credible sources that are the hallmark of academic writing and conversations. Your instructor will teach you strategies for determining if a source is credible, and he or she may have specific guidelines for the types of sources you are expected to use in your essays. Generally speaking, though, you can expect to learn how to find, integrate, and cite the following types of sources into your own writing (though you are certainly not limited to this list):

- ► Scholarly sources from peer-reviewed journals, including reports of scientific studies, experiments, or qualitative research (interviews, case studies, etc.)
- ► Scholarly or popular press books
- ► News reports from reputable journalism publications
- ► Analytical articles or essays from reputable journalism publications
- ► US Government reports, studies, or laws
- ► Organization Web sites devoted to specific professional, social, political, or health issues (e.g., National Society of Professional Engineers, American Heart Association)
- ► TED Talks delivered by experts or other documentary films or videos

Academic writers use many different types of sources including those above, but it's important to remember that expert writers use research to provide different types of information and evidence that they find from these sources. Often, students assume that when their instructors ask them to incorporate research into their essays, the instructors are looking for statistics. Sometimes statistics help develop a writer's essay, but sources can be used to provide different types of evidence that advance a writer's purpose in meaningful ways. Therefore, we encourage writing students to think broadly about the types of information that reliable sources can offer. For example, a student who was writing an essay exploring how workers are affected by automation (using robots and computers to complete tasks originally done by humans), could use a range of types of evidence to support the discussion as shown below:

| Types of Evidence | Examples |
|---|---|
| Facts or statistics | ▶ Identifying number of people laid off by automation in the last decade<br><br>▶ Citing the number of companies/industries that have shifted to automation in the last decade<br><br>▶ Quoting government unemployment statistics due to automation |
| Anecdotes | ▶ Describing the experiences of individuals who lost their jobs because their companies/factories shifted to automation models of production<br><br>▶ Quoting company officials explaining why they made the move to automation |
| Analogies | ▶ Comparing how workers in other countries have been affected by automation<br><br>▶ Comparing current automation trends to the effect of industrialization (such as in the auto industry) during the early twentieth century |
| Scientific study report | ▶ Explaining a study that examined the relationship between automation and unemployment<br><br>▶ Summarizing a study of a company that chose not to automate to understand how such a trend influences workers and company profits |
| Expert testimonial | ▶ Citing opinions or arguments from leading economists who study the effects of automation on labor markets and unemployment<br><br>▶ Quoting psychologists who study the impact of job loss on workers who were laid off because their jobs were no longer needed |

Although it would make sense for a writer to include statistical information or facts in an essay about automation and unemployment, it's clear that different types of evidence would add nuance, detail, and complexity to the writer's discussion of the topic. When you review the student writing in the *Guide,* pay attention not just to the types of sources that students used, but also *how* they used them. You'll see a range of sources used for a variety of purposes, and we encourage you to work toward that in your own writing, as well.

The benefits of information literacy go well beyond first-year writing classes. When you learn to include results from research into your writing effectively, you prepare yourself for success in later college work. Making good decisions about the sources you wish to cite and how that information helps you to accomplish your writing purpose helps you to be in control of your writing. Summarizing, paraphrasing, and quoting your sources effectively shows that you truly understand them. Citing and documenting your sources correctly proves not only that you understand your sources but also that you understand how academic writing works. It also helps you to avoid charges of plagiarism. When we work with sources, we have to take special care to make sure that readers know exactly what we are claiming as our own thinking and writing and exactly what came from someone else. We will resist discussing research, documentation, and plagiarism at great length here because all of that will be addressed far more extensively in your class. You must, however, be alert to the importance of using research material ethically in this course and throughout your college career.

## DOCUMENTING SOURCES

We have referred above to "documentation" of sources, which may be a new term for you. Basically, documentation means giving readers a very precise way to know exactly where you got your language and information and when exactly you are using language or information from your sources. For example, you might have seen books that had footnotes at the bottom of the page, linked to small numbers inserted into the discussion. Those footnotes "document" the source of the information.

To make that reference work easier to do, academic writers have created several carefully defined documentation styles, depending on the field or discipline in which they are writing. In the same way that there are (sometimes unstated) rules associated with texting or tweeting, scholars have developed rules about how academic conversations are conducted through writing, and these rules are articulated by documentation styles. Most writers in the humanities use the documentation system of the Modern Language Association (MLA style), and this is the documentation style used most often in first-year writing classes. Writers in the social sciences usually use the documentation system of the American Psychological Association (APA style), so some first-year writing classes use, or at least

*"Working on a works cited as you go along instead of all at the end like I did would be easier."*

—*Sammy M.*

permit, APA style. Both of these styles insert a brief citation to a source inside parentheses (often starting with an author's last name) within the body of an essay, and then add a list of sources at the end that readers can identify quickly by using the information in the parentheses. All of the sample essays in this book that cite sources use those documentation styles. If you have not worked with documentation very much, be sure to look at those examples so that you have a better idea of how they work.

You will likely learn several documentation styles during your college career. We understand that this variety of documentation styles can seem confusing, but please try to keep an open mind about them. By the time you are done with college, you will settle into some familiar styles for your work, and you will come to understand all the problems these documentation styles actually solve for you. There are good reasons for the differences between documentation styles, rooted in disciplinary practices and priorities. For now, you mainly need to remember that they are meant to be used precisely, and that their accurate use is your best method to avoid charges of plagiarism.

## AVOIDING PLAGIARISM

Certainly, you understand that you cannot have someone else do your writing for you or copy a paper and turn it in as your own. Most students also understand Grand Valley's policy forbidding submission of the same work in two different classes (including earlier high school classes)—unless you have permission from *both* instructors. Many first-year college students believe that as long as they avoid such extremely dishonest behavior, they cannot be accused of plagiarism; unfortunately, that belief is not correct.

Plagiarism is not simply a matter of dishonest intentions. Working with research sources requires writers to understand difficult aspects of plagiarism and make skilled, positive efforts to credit sources accurately and fully. Again, everyone knows that you cannot use the words of other writers without putting those words in quotation marks and giving the original writer credit. Many first-year students are surprised to find that, to avoid committing plagiarism, they also must do the following:

▶ Give credit to sources for their *information and ideas* as well as their words;

▶ Quote any exact language from the source, even only a few words at a time, when they use that language within their own sentences;

▶ Avoid using the same general sentence structure used by the source, except in exact and clearly marked quotations;

▶ Use their documentation style precisely to make perfectly clear when they are using material from a source and when they are presenting their own words and ideas.

You will learn more about documentation and avoiding plagiarism throughout your first-year writing class, so your instructor may continue to work with your drafts even if they contain sections that might commit intentional or unintentional plagiarism. If you want more information about why we do that, read the statement by the national Council of Writing Program Administrators (CWPA) about best approaches to working with students on the concept of plagiarism, found online at http://www.wpacouncil.org/positions/WPAplagiarism.pdf.

Furthermore, we may not always see when you are using material from sources while we are working on your drafts. We rely on you to inform us of that. Nevertheless, by the end of the course, in your final portfolio, we will check closely for plagiarism and hold you entirely accountable for it according to the Grand Valley Student Code. Thus, you need to be sure that you understand how to document all your sources before the end of this class. Be sure that you ask your instructor or consultants in the Writing Center about any instances of possible plagiarism in your work.

# FOCUSING ON REVISION: ONE STUDENT'S PROCESS

One of the most important skills you will practice and develop as a writing student this semester is your ability to revise your own writing. Revision is difficult—once we do the hard work of getting our ideas onto the page, it can be painful to change it, move it around, or worse, delete it. A novice writer is more likely to simply correct a few sentence-level errors and then call revision done; however, a more experienced writer knows that careful revision requires one to take a step back from the draft, look at the big picture, and ask important questions about purpose, audience, organization, and clarity. These questions might change the essay radically, but more often than not, the change is for the better because it helps the writer think more clearly about the message the audience needs to hear.

To help illustrate the types of radical revisions students do in first-year writing classes, we've selected an essay that Anna Wheeler wrote in Professor Stolley's class. Rather than showing you only the final product that Anna turned in at the end of the semester, we've collected two of her earlier drafts to show how her essay changed—and improved significantly—through revision. A marketing and human resources management major from Sparta, MI, Anna says that she's most proud of this essay, "The 'Wrong Kind' of Asian." The essay explores stereotypes against Asian Americans, and according to Anna, writing it allowed her to research and become more comfortable talking about her own experience and perspective as an Asian American with others.

Anna's first draft is a two-page exploration of her topic, and you'll see how her focus and purpose change as she continues writing, researching, and revising in subsequent drafts. You'll also see in her revised draft that she included notes to herself about ideas she knew she needed to develop and revise in further drafts. As we stated earlier, each writer's process is different, so we don't expect you all to follow Anna's exact model. However, by viewing this example, we think you and your classmates will be able to point out the specific revision strategies Anna used so that you might try them out in your own writing this semester.

**Anna's Advice for WRT 150 Students**

I believe students often get frustrated with finding a topic because they think their lives are "boring" and/or "not interesting enough." This is not true. Finding topics to write about is not easy, especially personal related ones. My advice is to find something that you consider a personal victory. No matter how small the accomplishment is, it could lead to a spark of new ideas. Another idea is to find something that has always bothered you. Jot down all of your feelings towards the topic and then go back and research to find more issues related to the topic. You will find much more information and learn that you are not alone on the idea.

# ANNA'S FIRST DRAFT

## The "Wrong Kind" of Asian

It seems that today, we are all assigned a label. This label is something we carry around with us for the rest of our lives. Many of us are often unhappy with the label we are given, and strive to change it throughout our times Due to my ethnicity, I have been labeled a "typical Asian" by my small community of prevalently white-race. When I step into bigger communities such as Grand Valley State University, the stereotype still follows me, wherever I go. The typical Asian stereotype seem to be stamped onto my forehead. Even though I was adopted by a white family, people continue to judge me off my looks. People assume several things about me, such as my smartness, my language I speak, and my economic success, all due to my looks. This stereotype comes from the "Model Minority" representation of Asian Americans, where their demographic profile speaks for the whole group. According to Taylor and Stern, Asian Americans are considered a "model minority" due to their affluence, high education, and managerial/ professional occupations- and rapid growth in number. The Model Minority theory ultimately dismantles Asians leaving them behind with a preconceived way of how they must function in life and provokes discriminating and racist behavior.

Similar to all other racial stereotypes, Asian Americans are subjected to a variety of stereotypes. Racial slang is often thrown in my face on the daily, yet sometimes I wonder where people are attaining their information from and if they fully understand what they are saying. Several of the Asian stereotypes that can used today, correlate with the events that have happened in the past. The Immigration Act of 1965, welcomed large numbers of Asians to enter the United States to work. Prior to this act, immigration into the US was regulated by the National Origins system, which "limited immigration from Asian to token levels" ("The 1965"). The new Immigration Act abolished restrictive quotas and relaxed the preference system. However, it only provided mass entry for those who fit the certain classes required of Asians. The requirement only allowed the wealthiest and educated from each Asian country into the US. After immigrating the certain classes, several professionals, scientists, technicians, graduate students, etc., where recruited to immigrate to the US. Policymakers sought this plan in order to fill scientific and technical positions that American students could not successfully fill. As a result, the immigration policy "controlled the quality of Asian immigrants in ways that they did not for other minorities" (Yen, 3). Thus, the inundation of successful Asians into America all at one time created a change in character for the Asian community, who were once viewed as "Yellow Peril", Asians viewed as aliens and a threat to wage-earners already in the US.

The emergence of the post-1965 Asian immigrants led to tensions between the old-time residents (US-born) and the new immigrated minority groups. The US-born citizens of the time accused many Asians of taking over and exploiting their communities. Several of the second-generation Asian Americans began working with the successful white Americans, which curated the white Americans ideas of Asian Americans as The Model Minority. The term "model minority" was first introduced in January 1966 in a New York Times Magazine by sociologist William Petersen. In his article, "Success story: Japanese American Style", the success of Japanese American is "quickly generalized across all Asian ethnic groups, regardless of their diversity in culture, education, and class" (Yoo). The success of appraised newly immigrated Asians appeared in numerous press articles. However, the Immigration Act of 1965 was often overlooked in Petersen's coining of "model minority". The lifting of restrictions and recruiting of professionals, is what ultimately created the large influx of successful Asian Americans. Petersen's term also concealed the discrepancies of other concepts, such as income, education, and health. The model minority term has led to the stereotyping of Asians that is now affecting current generations.

Paragraph 4—effects on communities
The Model Minority stereotype is proof that some racial stereotypes can seem favorable, however the people of the group can also be exploited in negative way. The model-minority image brings about a number of problems.

Paragraph 5—effects on communities
Paragraph 6—how it can be proven wrong
Paragraph 7—conclusion

*Word Count: 712*

# ANNA'S REVISED DRAFT

## The "Wrong Kind" of Asian

I am Asian. Growing up in a Caucasian-populated town, I am an easy target for bullies. I am always the odd one out. My outward appearances do not look like everyone else's. Not everyone accepts my nationality, but I am proud of it. As a young child, I never considered myself "different" from everyone else. My parents are both white. While I was growing up, they have always made me feel like I belonged. My point-of-view was changed when someone pointed out to me that I was different from everyone else. "Your eyes look different than mine" is the statement that started it all and still continues to be pointed out to me. I remember going home that night and wondering why my eyes were different from everyone else's. This was something I pondered over for several years. Why couldn't I just look like everyone else?

Racism isn't just black and white. The racist jokes I receive are usually all the same: "Open your eyes," "Go back to the rice picking fields," "You have to be smart . . . You're Asian." These stereotypes comes from the "Model Minority" representation of Asian Americans, where their demographic profile speaks for the whole group. According to Taylor and Stern, Asian Americans are considered a "model minority" due to their affluence, high education, and managerial/professional occupations- and rapid growth in number. The Model Minority theory leaves Asians behind with a preconceived way of how they must function in life and provokes discriminating and racist behavior.

Similar to all other racial stereotypes, Asian Americans are subjected to a variety of stereotypes. Racial slang is often thrown in my face on the daily, yet sometimes I wonder where people are attaining their information from and if they fully understand what they are saying. Several of the Asian stereotypes that can used today, correlate with the events that have happened in the past. The Immigration Act of 1965 welcomed large numbers of Asians to enter the United States to work. Prior to this act, immigration into the US was regulated by the National Origins system, which "limited immigration from Asian to token levels" ("The 1965"). The new Immigration Act abolished restrictive quotas and relaxed the preference system. However, it only provided mass entry for those who fit the certain classes required of Asians. The requirement only allowed the wealthiest and educated from each Asian country into the US. After immigrating, the certain classes, several professionals, scientists, technicians, graduate students, and others were recruited to immigrate to the US. Policymakers sought this plan in order to fill scientific and technical positions that American students could not successfully fill. As a result, the immigration policy "controlled the quality of Asian immigrants in ways that they did not for other minorities" (Yen 3). Thus, the inundation of successful Asians into America all at one time created a change in character for the Asian community, who were once viewed as "Yellow Peril", aliens and a threat to wage-earners already in the US.

The emergence of the post-1965 Asian immigrants led to tensions between the old-time residents (US-born) and the new immigrated minority groups. The US-born citizens of the time accused many Asians of taking over and exploiting their communities. Several of the second-generation Asian Americans began working with the successful white Americans, which curated the white Americans ideas of Asian Americans as The Model Minority. The term "model minority" was first introduced in January 1966 in a New York Times Magazine by sociologist William Petersen. In his article, "Success Story: Japanese American Style", the success of Japanese Americans is emphasized upon because _____ (Japanese were believed to be the clostest to Americans); thus, he "quickly generalized across all Asian ethnic groups, regardless of their diversity in culture, education, and class" (Yoo). The success of newly immigrated Asians appeared in numerous press articles. However, the Immigration Act of 1965 was often overlooked in Petersen's coining of "model minority". The lifting of restrictions and recruiting of professionals is what ultimately created the large influx of successful Asian Americans. Petersen's term also concealed the discrepancies of other concepts, such as income, education, and health. The model minority term has led to the stereotyping of Asians that is now affecting current generations.

The Model Minority stereotype is proof that some racial stereotypes can seem favorable, however the people of the group can also be exploited in negative way. The model-minority image brings about several problems. One of the major implications that arise is harsh stereotyping and discrimination. The way the media portrays the Asian American community encourages others to participate in the "typical Asian" stereotyping that leads to perceptions that all members of the community are alike. When ABC debuted its new sitcom in 2015 titled, Fresh Off the Boat, which featured an Asian American family, the cast was asked an offensive question during its open panel. The panel was asked "from an unknown reporter who said, 'I love the Asian culture. And I was just talking about the chopsticks, and I just love all that. Will I get to see that, or will it be more Americanized?'" (McRady). This goes to prove that the so called "outdated" stereotypes still exist and are repulsive throughout the media. The reporter ultimately reduced the entire Asian culture to chopsticks. Although much of the stereotyping of Asians are positive, they can still lead to several factors that ultimately leave the Asian community at disadvantage. A study was conducted that focused on Asian-American's participants ethnicity and was hypothesized to make them derive better test scores than those participants whose identities were not identified beforehand. However, the study resulted in, "under these conditions, ethnicity salience resulted in diminished ability to concentrate, which in turn led to significantly impaired math performance" (Cheryan). This research is crucial considering that people hold positive stereotypes over Asians and their mathematical skills. By doing so, this creates high pressure for the Asian community and can result in a negative performance on test.

Additionally, the Model Minority theory forces upon the idea that Asians are not outstanding communicators due to the language barrier and are therefore quiet and silent. However, this is affecting several Asian Americans and Pacific Islanders students in the classroom as this stereotypical image "may also pose pressure upon them to violate their cultural upbringing and conform to the Western norms in the classroom, where grades are often based upon students' verbal participation" (FIND AUTHOR). In result of conforming, this can conflictingly affect the relationship between parent and child of Asian ethnicity. Several Asian families come with their own ethics and morels; the Model Minority theory can put pressure onto young Asian students to change their ways in the classroom to what they were previously raised to do.

The Asian stereotype, mainly driven from the Model Minority Theory, that yet continues to thrive to its existence today, is often ignored because several people (outside of the Asian ethnicity) view the image as something "positive". The typical "smart Asian" stereotype leads everyone to conclude that if you're Asian, you must be smart. In turn, this puts a lot of pressure on Asians who are not "naturally smart" to attempt to live up to their standard or else face outside judgements. Many Asians feel that they are unable to create an image for themselves, but rather already have a template waiting for them to fill. The pressure to fill this template is discussed in Asian American Law Journal. Rhoda J. Yen mentioned Daya Sandhu, a Professsor of Educational and Counseling Psychology who explained that the social pressure to fulfill the "smart Asian" stereotype causes numerous "mental health concerns and psychological afflictions, such as threats to cultural identity, powerlessness, feelings of marginality, loneliness, hostility and perceived alienation and discrimination" (Rhoda). The amount of pressure on Asian Americans that is causing health problems is being hidden under the positive attributes that are ultimately just reinforcing racism.

*Note: (use as support- people see Asians as threat, thus the negativity towards them) people often feel realistic threat from groups that are perceived as model minorities such as Asian Americans. In other words, the perception that Asian Americans or other groups have certain model minority traits—including being hardworking, intelligent, and ambitious—leads to a sense that such groups pose a threat to other groups in terms of educational, economic, and political opportunities, and that such a sense of realistic threat may lead to negative attitudes and emotions. (Maddux).*

*(Option 2- Asian stereotypes being ignored)*

*They also argued that their experiences of racism and discrimination as a minority were often dismissed, as some people outside the group believed that —Asians are the new Whites [16] (p. 76). This is related to the model minority stereotype, which views AAPIs as privileged and accomplished.*

Similarly, the Georgia State University sociologist Rosalind Chou has found that the model-minority standard places enormous pressure on Asian Americans to disavow and downplay incidents of racial harassment; when Asian Americans are depicted as the minority group that doesn't complain, attract negative attention, or cause problems, it can feel uncomfortable for them to point out stereotypes, insults, and assaults. (The Atlantic).

"Asian Americans can also feel embarrassed to acknowledge failure to achieve certain academic or occupational achievements and thus do not seek help" (Zhen).

In addition to receiving racial hinders, Asian Americans are also affected by the Model Minority in institutional organizations such as the workplace and colleges. Although a majority of the Asian community has differing levels of college degrees, many of which are only being used at low-level jobs. An Asian American organization, ASCEND, collected data from HP, Intel, Google, LinkedIn, and Yahoo to show that within these top companies, Asian Americans represent 27% of professionals, 19% of managers, and just 14% of executives" (Chin). It was additionally calculated that "in these five firms, and white men and women are 154% more likely than Asians to hold an executive role" (Johnson). The Model Minority represents Asians as a group of hard working individuals who thrive to be successful and pass the work-ethic drive onto their offspring. The naturally "smart Asian" stereotype mentioned above, tends to follow Asians throughout their life, even in the professional field. So why aren't Asians advancing in the workplace? Jane Hyun explained the situation by coining the term "Bamboo Ceiling", similar to the "Glass Ceiling" effect. This term examines the level of diversity while climbing a corporate ladder. It can be seen in any business; the higher you climb, the less diversity is found. This can revert back to the stereotyping of Asians as poor communicators, which is a big turn off for a leadership position.

Another reason why Asian Americans may not be reaching the leadership spots in the professional workplace is due to college admissions. Much of the Asian population attend Ivy-League schools and elite universities nationwide and are continuing to overtake fields such as medicine, engineering, and computer science. However, their representation at Harvard University is steadily stable, with no increase or decrease. With the increase in population of Asian Americans rising sharply, there was much speculation for why Harvard's count for Asian Americans wasn't increasing. There is much speculation that Harvard has a quota in which they limit their Asian American representation and therefore reject several Asian students despite their top notch performances. According to Strauss, "many Asian-American students who have almost perfect SAT scores, top 1% GPAs, plus significant awards or leadership positions in various extracurricular activities have been rejected by Harvard University". In response, the Asian community filed a complaint against Harvard complaining that they are using racial quotas to admit students other than the Asians. While this is a severe problem, many Asian Americans are choosing to opt around this roadblock to their college admission. Brian Taylor, an Ivy league coach out of Manhattan, is directing his clients to not check "Asian" when applying for colleges as this makes the student appear "less Asian" and therefore appear as just a "normal" smart student. This is creating a strain on Asian students as they have their future to worry for due to their ethnicity.

(Asians in the workplace- less higher up positions due to COLLEGE admissions)

"Since the Ivies produce a disproportionate number of CEOs, Congressmen and judges, the apparent bias against Asian-Americans at leading universities may also keep Asians out of leadership spots. "The ladder is being pulled away from our feet," says Tricia Liu. "If we can't go to the Ivy League universities, how can we get the positions in Wall Street, or Congress, or the Supreme Court?"("Model Minority...")

Despite the Model Minority theory that has wound the world's brain around the stereotypes of Asians, this model seems to be more of a myth than something to follow. The Model Minoirty isolates the Asian populations in a way that can tragically hurt them. It creates high expecatations that can be proven wrong. The Model Minority myth presents Asians as successful in their careers with a financially stable background. When examining the poverty rates in 2007-2011 published by the US Census, Asian Americans ranked one of the lowest poverty rates according to race at 12.8%., with whites ranking comparably (Macartney). However, when looking closer at the data, Asian Americans were experiencing the fastest growth in poverty rates in the United States. According to the Center for American Progress, during the same term of 2007-2011, the povery level for Asian Americans increased by 37%, which surpasses the US national increase of 27% (Ramakrishnan). Another conclusion that come from the Model Minority effect is that Asians are taking over America. While the population of Asian's in America is dramatically increasing, the etimatin on the net effect of immigration is not taking into account different factors. The net effect of immigration status for Asian Americans is "unwarranted for Asian Americans because it is based on studies that mostly compare native-born whites with foreign-born Asian Americans" (Sakamoto). This conclusion does not differentiate a net immigration effect from a new racial effect. (insert more facts?)

Overall, the Model Minority theory is penalizing Asians of a preconceived way to which they must function in life and is encouraging discriminating and racist behavior from outside sources. Many seem to believe that everything about the Asian stereotype is "positive" so it's not really a problem. However, what people seem to forget is the indivuals in the Asian community are not all one. Not every Asian is having the "smart Asian" effect, or derives from a "wealthy, successful" family. By grouping an entire ethnic population into one and assuming they all function the same, puts a strain on the individuals to live up to their expectations. In turn, this also shames those who stand different from the group, such as those who aren't as smart in school, or aren't the typical "quiet nerd". The Model Minority theory is a myth and what is important to attain is that just like every ethnicity, there will be people who are very successful, but there are also those who are still living on the streets trying to make it on their own.

*Word Count: 2523*

Works Cited

Maddux, William W., et al. "When being a Model Minority is Good
. and Bad: Realistic Threat Explains Negativity Toward Asian
Americans." Personality and Social Psychology Bulletin, vol.
34, no. 1, 2008, pp. 74-89, doi:10.1177/0146167207309195.

Cheryan, Sapna, and Galen V. Bodenhausen. "When Positive
Stereotypes Threaten Intellectual Performance: The
Psychological Hazards of "Model Minority" Status."
Psychological Science, vol. 11, no. 5, 2000, pp. 399-402,
doi:10.1111/1467-9280.00277.

Zhen, Anna. "A Review of the Negative Effects of Seemingly
Positive Stereotyping of Asians and Asian Americans on
Their Academic Performance and Health." JOURNAL OF
PSYCHOLOGY (2016): 23.

Strauss, Valerie. Asian Americans File Complaint Alleging
Discrimination in Harvard Admissions. WP Company LLC
d/b/a The Washington Post, Washington, 2015.

"Does the 'Bamboo Ceiling' Shut Asian Americans Out of Top
Jobs?", National Public Radio, 2014.

Johnson, Stephanie. https://hbr.org/2016/12/why-arent-there-more-
asian-americans-in-leadership-positions

Chin, Margaret M. "Asian Americans, Bamboo Ceilings, and
Affirmative Action." Contexts, vol. 15, no. 1, 2016, pp. 70-73,
doi:10.1177/1536504216628845.

Rhoda J. Yen, "Racial Stereotyping of Asians and Asian Americans
and Its Effect on Criminal Justice: A Reflection on the Wayne
Lo Case," 7

Asian Am. L.J. 1 (2000). Available at: http://scholarship.law.
berkeley.edu/aalj/vol7/iss1/1

Macartney, Suzanne. https://www.census.gov/prod/2013pubs/
acsbr11-17.pdf

Sakamoto, Arthur, et al. "The Myth of the Model Minority Myth."
Sociological Spectrum, vol. 32, no. 4, 2012, pp. 309-321, doi:
10.1080/02732173.2012.664042.

Ramakrishnan, Karthick, et. Al. https://cdn.americanprogress.org/
wp-content/uploads/2014/08/AAPI-IncomePoverty.pdf

# ANNA'S FINAL REVISION

## The "Wrong Kind" of Asian

I am Asian. Growing up in a Caucasian-populated town, I am an easy target for bullies. I am always the odd one out. My outward appearance does not look like everyone else's. Not everyone accepts my nationality, but I am proud of it. As a young child, I never considered myself "different." My parents are both white. While I was growing up, they have always made me feel like I belonged. My point-of-view was changed when someone pointed out to me that I was different from everyone else. "Your eyes look different than mine" is the statement that started it all and continues to be pointed out to me. I remember going home that night and wondering why my eyes were different from everyone else's. This was something I pondered over for several years. Why was I continuously criticized for something so inconsequential?

The racist jokes I receive are usually all the same: "Open your eyes," "Go back to the rice picking fields," "You have to be smart... You're Asian." The last comment is a stereotype that derives from the "Model Minority" representation of Asian Americans, which perceives the overall Asian American race as socioeconomically successful over all other groups. According to Taylor and Stern, both who are Professors in the US, Asian Americans are considered a "model minority" due to their "affluence, high education, and managerial/professional occupations- and rapid growth in number". The Model Minority theory leaves Asians behind with a preconceived way of how they must function in life and provokes discriminating and racist behavior.

Similar to all other racial stereotypes, Asian Americans are subjected to a variety of stereotypes. Racial slang is often thrown in my face on the daily, yet sometimes I wonder where people are attaining their information from and if they fully understand what they are saying. Several of the Asian stereotypes that are used today correlate with the events that have happened in the past. The Immigration Act of 1965 welcomed large numbers of Asians to enter the United States to work. Before this act, immigration into the US was regulated by the National Origins system, which "limited immigration from Asian to token levels" ("Origins"). The new

Immigration Act abolished restrictive quotas and relaxed the preference system. A new wave of Asians who were previously denied access were now allowed to immigrate to the US. However, it only provided mass entry for those who fit the certain classes required of Asians. The requirement only allowed the wealthiest and educated from each Asian country into the US. After immigrating the certain classes, others who did not fit into these were then recruited to immigrate to the US. The wealthiest/ most educated were drafted first, and then others were recruited. Policymakers sought this plan to fill scientific and technical positions that American students could not successfully fill. As a result, the immigration policy "controlled the quality of Asian immigrants in ways that they did not for other minorities" (Yen 3). Thus, the inundation of successful Asians into America all at one time created a change in character for the Asian community, who were once viewed as aliens and a threat to wage-earners already in the US.

The rise in Asian immigrants created strains between the original American occupants and the newly moved minority group. The American citizens immediately blamed many Asians for assuming control and taking over their communities. Several of the second-generation Asian Americans began working with the successful white Americans, which curated the white Americans ideas of Asian Americans as The Model Minority. The term "model minority" was first introduced in January 1966 in a *New York Times Magazine* by sociologist William Petersen. In his article, "Success Story: Japanese American Style," the success of Japanese Americans is emphasized upon because the Japanese were thought to be the closest related to Americans; thus, several people "quickly generalized across all Asian ethnic groups, regardless of their diversity in culture, education, and class" (Yoo). The success of newly immigrated Asians appeared in numerous press articles. However, the Immigration Act of 1965 was often overlooked in Petersen's coining of "model minority." The lifting of restrictions and recruiting of professionals is what ultimately created the large influx of successful Asian Americans. Petersen's term also concealed the discrepancies of other concepts, such as income, education, and health. The model minority term has led to the stereotyping of Asians that is now affecting current generations.

The Model Minority stereotype is proof that some racial stereotypes can seem favorable. However, the people of the group can also be exploited in a negative way. The model-minority image brings about several problems. One of the major implications that arise is harsh stereotyping and discrimination. The Model Minority theory has created several stereotypes that create a generalization across all Asian Americans, despite the multiple different backgrounds that they come from. Although much of the stereotyping of Asians are positive and can seem like a compliment to those outside of the ethnicity, much of the assumptions can be harmful. Considering all Asians as "successful" and "hardworking" does not bring to truth the factors that ultimately leaves the Asian community at disadvantage by lumping the entire ethnic group into one stereotype. A study was conducted that focused on Asian-American participants' ethnicity and was hypothesized to make them derive better test scores than those participants whose identities were not acknowledged beforehand. The study predicted that by making the ethnicity salient before taking the test, there would be an enhanced test score from Asians in particular. However, the study resulted in, "under these conditions, ethnicity salience resulted in diminished ability to concentrate, which in turn led to significantly impaired math performance" (Cheryan and Bodenhausen 1). This research is crucial considering that people hold positive stereotypes over Asians and their mathematical skills. By doing so, this creates high pressure for the Asian community and can result in a negative performance on a test, which may affect the future for the new generation.

Additionally, the Model Minority theory forces upon the idea that Asians are not outstanding communicators due to the language barrier and are therefore quiet and silent. However, this is affecting several Asian Americans and Pacific Islander students in the classroom as this stereotypical image "may also pose pressure upon them to violate their cultural upbringing and conform to the Western norms in the classroom, where grades are often based upon students' verbal participation" (Kwon et al. 10). In result of conforming, this can conflictingly affect the relationship between parent and child of Asian ethnicity. Several Asian families come with their ethics and morals. The Model Minority theory can put pressure on young Asian students to change their ways in the classroom from what they were previously raised to do.

The Asian stereotypes that are driven from the Model Minority Theory are often ignored because several people outside of the

Asian ethnicity view the image as something "positive." The typical "smart Asian" stereotype leads everyone to conclude that if you're Asian, you must be smart. In turn, this puts a lot of pressure on Asians who are not "naturally smart" to attempt to live up to their standard or else face outside judgment. Many Asians feel that they are unable to create an image for themselves, but rather already have a template waiting for them to fill. The pressure to fill this template is discussed in *Asian American Law Journal*. Daya Sandhu, a Professor of Educational and Counseling Psychology, explained that the social pressure to fulfill the "smart Asian" stereotype causes numerous "mental health concerns and psychological afflictions, such as threats to cultural identity, powerlessness, feelings of marginality, loneliness, hostility and perceived alienation and discrimination" (qtd. in Yen 6). Since the stereotype is prevalent to much of society, Asians often take the racism that is handed to them. Current research by William Maddux, a professor at INSEAD, tried to explain the reasoning for the stereotyping. The research demonstrates that the Asian American perception created by the Model Minority theory creates a sense of threat and competition to other groups regarding economic-wise, which in turn may lead to the negative attitudes and emotions towards the Asians (Maddux et al. 1). This reasoning demonstrates that people are unaware of the diverse ethnic identity and background that appears within the Asian American group, and therefore make assumptions from an outdated myth.

In addition to receiving racial hinders, Asian Americans are also affected by the Model Minority in institutional organizations such as the workplace and college. Although a majority of the Asian community has differing levels of college degrees, many are only being used for low-level jobs. An Asian American organization, ASCEND, collected data from HP, Intel, Google, LinkedIn, and Yahoo to show that within these top companies, "Asian Americans represent 27% of professionals, 19% of managers, and just 14% of executives" (Chin). It was additionally calculated that "in these five firms, white men and women are 154% more likely than Asians to hold an executive role" (Johnson and Sy 1). The Model Minority represents Asians as a group of hardworking individuals who thrive to be successful and pass the work-ethic drive onto their offspring. The naturally "smart Asian" stereotype mentioned above, tends to follow Asians throughout their life, even in the professional field. So why aren't Asians advancing in the workplace? Jane Hyun explained the situation by coining the term "Bamboo Ceiling," similar to the "Glass Ceiling" effect (Chen). This term examines the level of diversity while climbing the corporate ladder. It can be seen in any business; the higher you climb, the less diversity is found. This can revert to the stereotyping of Asians as poor communicators, which is a big turn off for a leadership position.

Another reason why Asian Americans may not be reaching the leadership spots in the professional workplace is due to college admissions. Much of the Asian population attends Ivy-League schools and elite universities nationwide and are continuing to overtake fields such as medicine, engineering, and computer science. However, their representation at Harvard University is solidly stable, with no increase or decrease. With the increase in the population of Asian Americans rising sharply, there is much speculation for why Harvard's count for Asian Americans isn't increasing. It is believed that Harvard has a quota in which they limit their Asian American representation and therefore reject several Asian students despite their top-notch performances. According to Valerie Strauss, a Washington DC reporter, "many Asian-American students who have almost perfect SAT scores, top 1% GPAs, plus significant awards or leadership positions in various extracurricular activities have been rejected by Harvard University" (Strauss). In response, the Asian community filed a complaint against Harvard complaining that they are using racial quotas to admit students other than the Asians. While this is a severe problem, many Asian Americans are choosing to opt around this roadblock to their college admission. Brian Taylor, an Ivy League coach out of Manhattan, is directing his clients not to check "Asian" when applying for colleges as this makes the student appear "less Asian" and therefore appear as just a "normal" smart student (English). This is creating a strain on Asian students as they have their future to worry for due to their ethnicity.

Despite the Model Minority theory that has created the strong stereotypes of Asians, this model seems to be more of a myth than something to follow. The Model Minority isolates the Asian population in a way that can tragically hurt them. It creates high expectations that can be proven wrong. The Model Minority myth presents Asians as successful in their careers with a financially stable background. When examining the poverty rates in 2007-2011 published by the US Census, Asian Americans ranked one of the lowest poverty rates according to race at 12.8%, with whites ranking comparable (Macartney et al. 1). However, when looking closer at the data, Asian Americans were experiencing the fastest growth in poverty rates in the United States. According to the Center for American Progress, during the same term of 2007-2011, the poverty level for Asian Americans increased by 37%, which surpasses the US national increase of 27% (Ramakrishnan and Ahmad). Another conclusion that comes from the Model Minority effect is that Asians are taking over America. While the population of Asians in America is dramatically increasing, the estimation of the net effect of immigration is not taking into account the different factors. The net effect of immigration status for Asian Americans is being mistaken as "the difference in means between a group of immigrants and a group of non-immigrants who are otherwise similar" (Sakamoto et al. 312). This conclusion does not differentiate a net immigration effect from a new racial effect. The Asian stereotype is created by dismissing various aspects and jumping straight to conclusions.

Overall, the Model Minority theory is penalizing Asians of a preconceived way to which they must function in life and is encouraging discriminating and racist behavior from outside sources. However, the Model Minority theory is negatively affecting the Asian American population in the US, rather than helping them. The racist stereotyping that is derived from the theory is leading to poor performance on tests due to the high pressure the stereotype holds upon Asians. Additionally, the Model Minority theory is affecting Asian Americans' ability to get into Ivy League schools and move up corporate ladders in their careers. Given my Asian ethnicity, I have yet to experience any negative effects of the Model Minority stereotype. However, this still directly affects me as I head into my future knowing that I may be at an unfair advantage due the color of my face and the shape of my eyes. Looking forward, I hope to see a future with no stereotypes based on the Model Minority theory as this is simply a myth that has evolved into a generalization of an entire ethnic population.

*Word Count: 2308*

Works Cited

Chen, Liyan. "How Asian Americans Can Break Through the Bamboo Ceiling." *Forbes,* 20 Jan. 2016, www.forbes.com/sites/liyanchen/2016/01/20/how-asian-americans-can-break-through-the-bamboo-ceiling/#1791cc0b1e43

Cheryan, Sapna, and Galen V. Bodenhausen. "When Positive Stereotypes Threaten Intellectual Performance: The Psychological Hazards of 'Model Minority' Status." *Psychological Science*, vol. 11, no. 5, Sep. 2000, pp 399-402, *Sage Journals*, doi:10.1111/1467-9280.00277.

Chin, Margaret M. "Asian Americans, Bamboo Ceilings, and Affirmative Action." Contexts, vol. 15, no. 1, 2016, pp. 70-73, *Sage Journals,* doi:10.1177/1536504216628845.

English, Bella. "To get into Elite Colleges, Some Advised to 'Appear Less Asian'." *Boston Globe*, Boston Glove Media Partners, LLC, 01 June 2015, www.bostonglobe.com/lifestyle/2015/06/01/college-counselors-advise-some-asian-students-appear-less-asian/Ew7g4JiQMiqYNQlIwqEIuO/story.html

Johnson, Stephanie, and Thomas Sy. "Why Aren't There More Asian Americans in Leadership Positions?" *Harvard Business Review*, Harvard Business Publishing, 19 Dec. 2016, hbr.org/2016/12/why-arent-there-more-asian-americans-in-leadership-positions

Kwon, Jimin, et al. "Stereotype Threat on Asian American College Students." *Advanced Science and Technology Letters*, vol. 59, 2014, pp. 7-13, dx.doi.org/10.14257/astl.2014.59.02

Macartney, Suzanne, et. al. "Poverty Rates for Selected Detailed Race and Hispanic Groups by State and Place: 2007-2011." US Census Bureau, American Community Survey, 2007-2011. Feb. 2013. www.census.gov/prod/2013pubs/acsbr11-17.pdf

Maddux, William W., et al. "When being a Model Minority is Good… and Bad: Realistic Threat Explains Negativity Toward Asian Americans." *Personality and Social Psychology Bulletin*, vol. 34, no. 1, Sage Publications, 2008, pp. 74-89, *Sage Journals* doi:10.1177/0146167207309195.

"Origins of the 1965 Immigration Act." *The 1965 Immigration Act: Asian-Nation*, www.asian-nation.org/1965-immigration-act.shtml.

Ramakrishnan, Karthick, and Farah Z. Ahmad. "Income and Poverty: Part of the 'State of Asian Americans and Pacific Islanders' Series." *Center for American Progress*, 21 July 2014. cdn.americanprogress.org/wp-content/uploads/2014/08/AAPI-IncomePoverty.pdf

Sakamoto, Arthur, et al. "The Myth of the Model Minority Myth." *Sociological Spectrum*, vol. 32, no. 4, Taylor and Francis Group2012, pp. 309-321, *EBSCOhost*, doi:10.1080/02732173.2012.664042.

Strauss, Valerie. "Asian Americans File Complaint Alleging Discrimination in Harvard Admissions." *The Washington Post*, 16 May 2015, www.washingtonpost.com/news/answer-sheet/wp/2015/05/16/asian-americans-file-complaint-alleging-discrimination-in-harvard-admissions/?utm_term=.dc64d3780dbf

Taylor, Charles R., and Barbara B. Stern. "Asian-Americans: Television Advertising and the 'Model Minority' Stereotype." *Journal of Advertising*, vol. 26, no. 2, Taylor and Francis Ltd, 1997, *Michigan Library*, www.jstor.org/stable/4189033

Yen, Rhoda J. "Racial Stereotyping of Asians and Asian Americans and Its Effect on Criminal Justice: A Reflection on the Wayne Lo Case," *Asian American Law Journal*, vol. 7, no. 1, pp. 1-28, scholarship.law.berkeley.edu/aalj/vol7/iss1/1

Yoo, Brandon. "Unraveling the Model Minority Myth of Asian American Students." *Education.com*, 25 Oct. 2010, www.education.com/reference/article/unraveling-minority-myth-asian-students/.

# UNIVERSITY AND WRITING DEPARTMENT POLICIES

First-year writing classes at Grand Valley can have many differences in terms of assignments, daily routines, and instruction. We want all instructors to teach in the ways that best suit their abilities and the needs of their particular students. Nevertheless, as part of our effort to ensure consistency across sections, all instructors adhere to the following university and departmental policies.

## REQUIRED PASSING GRADE

You must pass WRT 130 or WRT 150 with a grade of C or better (above C–) to satisfy Grand Valley's General Education Foundation—Writing requirement. If you do not receive a grade of C or better, you will need to take WRT 130 or WRT 150 again.

## LEARNING OR PHYSICAL DISABILITIES

If you have any special needs because of learning, physical, or any other disabilities, please contact Disability Support Resources at 616-331-2490. Any student needing academic accommodations beyond those given to the entire class needs to request assistance from DSR. Writing faculty work with DSR to accommodate students' special needs and devise a plan that is fair to all students. Furthermore, if you have a disability and think you will need assistance evacuating a classroom and/or building in an emergency situation, please make your instructor and DSR aware so that Grand Valley can develop a plan to assist you.

## ATTENDANCE

Regular, timely, and full attendance is required to succeed in your first-year writing class. According to the Grand Valley catalog, instructors may fail students for excessive absences. In first-year writing classes, missing class more than four times constitutes excessive absences, and can be grounds for failing the course. Tardiness, leaving class while it is in session, coming unprepared, or off-task behavior (like texting) may also count as an absence or partial absence according to your instructor's policies. You might receive an e-mail warning from your instructor after the fourth absence, but it is your responsibility to keep track of your attendance. Excessive absence itself is the grounds for failure, so that lack of warning does not excuse any further absences. The warning simply provides additional clarity.

# THE FIRST-YEAR WRITING PORTFOLIO

People in a range of professional fields use portfolios to show other people what they are capable of producing. Your first-year writing portfolio represents your own end-of-semester writing capabilities. The portfolio includes three fully revised and polished papers, including at least one that integrates outside sources and accurately credits the ideas and language drawn from those sources. Together, these three pieces of writing produce your final letter grade.

The three papers in your portfolio represent your abilities as a college-level academic writer, so you should select and revise them with care. For example, you probably do not want three very short papers, since that would fail to show your ability to write a longer paper. Ask your instructor and peer reviewers about your selections if you are not sure. Your instructor and the other students can help you make good choices about what goes in the final portfolio. Also, read the full portfolios published in this book, and, together with your instructor and classmates, try to learn from them what makes a first-year writing portfolio successful.

**So that your instructor has time to check all work for any problems, we strictly enforce your instructor's requirements for turning in earlier versions of work that you intend to place in your portfolio.** All papers in your portfolio must have been assigned for the class and seen by your instructor in draft form before final submission.

## CHARACTERISTICS OF A, B, C, AND D PORTFOLIOS

We provide the general characteristics of A, B, and C portfolios for you here so that you can identify precisely how your work is evaluated. Characteristics that cause portfolios to fall below the standard for a passing grade are presented as characteristics of D papers. Factors that can cause you to receive an F for the course are listed at the end of the grading criteria. Your instructor, with the help of the instructor's portfolio grading group, will develop more specific understandings of these criteria to apply to your exact assignments and portfolios; in doing so, however, all of them will be seeking to apply the general characteristics accurately and fairly to your work.

## Characteristics of A Portfolios

### Content and Research

- ▶ The portfolio consistently engages the interest of intelligent and sophisticated college-level readers.
- ▶ Papers effectively address and engage their likely and intended audiences.
- ▶ Papers succeed at accomplishing challenging purposes.
- ▶ Each paper maintains a consistent focus on the main claim or goal for the paper.
- ▶ Each paper develops its focus with significant and interesting discussion, details, and examples, including graphics when useful.
- ▶ The portfolio clearly demonstrates the writer's information literacy and ability to use college-level academic research as a significant means to develop the writer's complex ideas.
- ▶ The portfolio clearly demonstrates the writer's ability to introduce and integrate material from relevant outside sources to advance the purposes for the writing and meet the expectations of intelligent and sophisticated college-level readers.

### Organization

- ▶ Titles and opening sections of papers inform readers appropriately of the topic, purpose, and focus of the paper in ways that motivate readers to continue reading.
- ▶ Paragraphs are purposefully organized and substantially developed with supporting evidence, examples, and reasoning.
- ▶ Paragraphs break information into parts that contribute to a greater understanding of the whole.
- ▶ Readers can easily see how the order in which information appears supports the focus and purpose of the papers.
- ▶ The papers lead readers through the order of the discussion in ways that are explicit, clear, and purposeful, including effective transition devices when needed.
- ▶ Readers can see a meaningful pattern in the order of the information as a whole.
- ▶ Closing sections give readers a satisfied sense that the purpose of the writing has been achieved.

### Style

- ▶ Word choice is precise, interesting, and appropriate to the writing purpose and audience.
- ▶ Language is mature and purposefully controlled.
- ▶ Sentences are clear, logical, enjoyable, and easily understood by college-level readers.
- ▶ Sentences often make active statements and use efficient and effective modification.
- ▶ Sentence structure varies according to the content, purpose, and audience.
- ▶ A consistent voice complements each paper's purpose, fits its genre, and appeals to its likely and intended readers.
- ▶ Information and quotations from sources are integrated skillfully into the writer's own sentences and paragraphs.

### Mechanics

- ▶ Format is consistent with the detailed requirements of an applicable style guide, such as the MLA or APA style guides.
- ▶ References to outside sources are cited and documented according to the appropriate style guide carefully enough that readers can easily identify the sources that have been quoted or referenced.
- ▶ Problems in grammar, spelling, punctuation, or usage do not interfere with communication.
- ▶ Editing shows effective attention to the desire of readers to read without being interrupted by unexpected errors or problems with documentation and format.

# Characteristics of B Portfolios

## *Content and Research*

- ▸ The portfolio connects with the interest of intelligent and sophisticated college-level readers.
- ▸ Papers clearly address the expectations of their likely and intended audiences.
- ▸ Papers accomplish or make strong attempts to accomplish challenging purposes.
- ▸ Each paper maintains a consistent, single focus.
- ▸ Each paper develops a focus with fitting and relevant discussions, details, and examples, including graphics when useful.
- ▸ The portfolio demonstrates the writer's ability to use college-level academic research clearly and purposefully to develop the writer's ideas.
- ▸ The portfolio demonstrates the writer's ability to introduce and integrate material from relevant outside sources in ways that enhance the accomplishment of goals and purposes.

## *Organization*

- ▸ Titles and opening sections of papers are well-chosen and appropriate to the topic and focus of the papers.
- ▸ Paragraphs are clearly organized and adequately developed with supporting evidence, examples, and reasoning, though some paragraphs may lack richness of detail or evidence.
- ▸ Paragraphs break information into parts that make sense and assist effective reading.
- ▸ Readers can identify the focus of each paper and follow it through the entire discussion.
- ▸ Readers can identify how the order in which information appears supports the focus and purpose of the papers.
- ▸ Overall patterns in the order of presentation make sense.
- ▸ Transitions between and within paragraphs advance the writer's ideas.
- ▸ Closing sections give readers a clear sense that the writer is ending the discussion at a good place.

## *Style*

- ▸ Word choice is generally appropriate to the writing purpose and audience.
- ▸ Language is generally mature and purposefully controlled.
- ▸ Sentences are generally clear, logical, and readable.
- ▸ Sentences typically make active statements, extended by efficient and effective modification.
- ▸ Sentences vary in structure and only occasionally are choppy, rambling, or repetitive.
- ▸ The voice in each paper is consistent and appropriate for the writer's genre, purpose, and audience.
- ▸ Information and quotations from sources make sense within the writer's own sentences and paragraphs.

## *Mechanics*

- ▸ Format is appropriate and generally follows the requirements of an assigned style guide, such as MLA or APA.
- ▸ References to outside sources are cited and documented according to the appropriate style guide carefully enough that readers can determine when source material has been used and find the sources.
- ▸ Mistakes in grammar, spelling, punctuation, or usage rarely interfere with communication.
- ▸ Editing shows attention to the desire of readers to read without being interrupted by unexpected errors.

# Characteristics of C Portfolios

## *Content and Research*

▶ The portfolio makes sense to intelligent and sophisticated college-level readers, though it may not consistently hold their interest.

▶ The portfolio presents ideas and descriptions with readers in mind.

▶ Papers appear to aim at accomplishing purposes.

▶ Each paper generally maintains a single focus, though the focus may be on a topic or an event rather than an idea, claim, or goal.

▶ Each paper generally develops a focus with details, examples, and discussions, including graphics when useful.

▶ The portfolio demonstrates the writer's ability to use relevant college-level academic research as a means to discuss a topic.

▶ The portfolio demonstrates the writer's ability to include material from outside sources within the general requirements of an applicable style guide.

## *Organization*

▶ Titles and openings generally match the topic and focus.

▶ Paragraphs make sense and usually use some evidence or detailed examples to support points.

▶ Papers generally establish an overall organizational pattern for readers to follow.

▶ Each paper develops a basic focus, with few paragraphs appearing to be out of sequence or off-track.

▶ Transitions from one section and idea to another are evident and make sense.

## *Style*

▶ Most words appear to be well chosen and fit the purpose and audience for the particular paper.

▶ Some of the sentences are short and choppy, long and rambling, vague and wordy, or repetitive.

▶ Sentences are generally readable and make sense.

▶ Sentences sometimes feature the efficient and effective uses of modifying clauses and phrases.

▶ The writer's voice is usually consistent and appropriate, fitting the writer's genre, purpose, and audience.

▶ Information and quoted language from sources is clearly presented as source material.

## *Mechanics*

▶ Format choices are generally appropriate for the purposes of the papers.

▶ References to outside sources are generally cited and documented, if not always in the appropriate style; readers can determine when source material has been quoted or referenced, and instances of unreferenced source material are few and clearly not intentional.

▶ Mistakes in grammar, spelling, punctuation, or usage do not generally interfere with either the writer's credibility or the reader's ability to read the text easily.

▶ Editing shows adequate attention to the desire of readers to read without being interrupted by unexpected errors.

# Characteristics of D Portfolios

## Content and Research

► Topics, purposes, claims, or focuses are so simplistic and obvious that they do not engage the interest of college-educated readers.
► Papers have no apparent and appropriate audiences.
► Papers have no clear purposes.
► At least one paper is clearly fictional.
► Papers lack a single focus.
► Ideas are stated, but they are not developed with details, examples, and discussions.
► Language and material from sources are consistently presented in ways that are very hard to follow.
► Unintentional, careless misuse of source material would amount to plagiarism had it been intentional.
► The portfolio shows weak research and information literacy skills, such as the use of very few sources, little variety of sources, or little obvious effort to conduct scholarly or professional research.
► Sources do not support and may even contradict the views that the writer attributes to them.

## Organization

► Openings and endings are missing, misleading, or overly general.
► Readers cannot readily see the focus of the papers.
► Paragraphs frequently seem unrelated to each other or repetitive.
► Paragraphs do not develop logically from start to finish, or they break in illogical places.
► Paragraphs often end without developing broad, general statements with evidence and reasoning.
► Transitions between and within paragraphs are weak, ineffective, or misleading.
► The papers do not establish clear patterns for readers to follow.

## Style

► Sentences are often short and choppy, long and rambling, vague and wordy, or repetitive.
► Disordered sentence parts, poor phrasing, and poor word choices make reading difficult.
► Sentences often disregard the normal rules of standard written English in ways that make ideas hard to understand.
► The voice often appears inappropriate for the writer's purpose, genre, and audience.

## Mechanics

► Format, including any use of graphics, is extremely careless or entirely disregards the basic requirements of applicable style guides.
► Language or material from outside sources is not clearly cited.
► Documentation style is generally wrong according to the assigned style guide, often in ways that interfere with readers' abilities to find the source material and locate the referenced portions of the sources.
► Instances of misused source material show careless inattention to important requirements for quoting, paraphrasing, and citing, raising questions of possible plagiarism.
► Many errors in spelling, grammar, punctuation, word choice, and usage make reading difficult, or they strongly limit the writer's credibility.

Regardless of overall student writing ability, portfolios will receive the grade of D if, as a whole, the portfolio fails to demonstrate that the student understands how to conduct college-level research as well as how to integrate the results of his/her research into purposeful writing without committing plagiarism. Otherwise, D portfolios rarely have similar characteristics. The lists below present the characteristics that help predict when a portfolio does not demonstrate competence. **The main key to avoiding a D is to meet the criteria for at least a C.**

## F Grades

The grade of F in first-year writing is reserved for the following circumstances:

- ▶ The student did not turn in a portfolio by the last day of class (or the due date set by the instructor's syllabus, if the instructor chooses another due date).
- ▶ The portfolio did not have three papers in it that qualified for the portfolio under this Guide and the instructor's syllabus.
- ▶ The student violated course polices set by this Guide or the instructor's syllabus (for example, an attendance policy), if the information made clear that the violation would result in a grade of F.
- ▶ The student violated other policies of Grand Valley State University that clearly state that the violation could result in a grade of F.
- ▶ The student clearly committed plagiarism, as described by Grand Valley's Student Code, this Guide, and the instructor's syllabus.
- ▶ The portfolio clearly demonstrates a complete indifference to earning any higher grade.

On the next few pages, you'll see the same portfolio characteristics you just read presented another way. This chart allows you to compare the differences for each grade level for the different criteria we will look at when we evaluate your drafts and final essays.

## CONTENT AND RESEARCH

| A Paper Characteristics | B Paper Characteristics | C Paper Characteristics | D Paper Characteristics |
|---|---|---|---|
| **Content:** consistently engages interest of intelligent, sophisticated college-level readers (intended audience); accomplishes challenging purposes. | **Content:** connects with intelligent, sophisticated college-level readers; clearly addresses audience's expectations; accomplishes or makes strong attempt to accomplish challenging purposes. | **Content:** makes sense to intelligent, sophisticated college-level readers, though may not hold interest consistently; presents ideas and descriptions with audience in mind; appears to aim at accomplishing a purpose. | **Content:** topics, purposes, claims, or focus are so simple and obvious that they fail to engage interest of college-level reader; no apparent and appropriate audience; no clear purpose; at least one paper in portfolio is clearly fictional. |
| **Focus:** maintained on main claim/goal; developed with significant, interesting discussion, details, and examples (including graphics when useful). | **Focus:** consistent and single focus; developed with fitting/relevant discussions, details, and examples (including graphics when useful). | **Focus:** maintains single focus, though might be on a topic/event rather than an idea, claim, or goal; generally develops focus with details, examples, and discussions (including graphics when useful). | **Focus:** lacks single focus; ideas are stated but not developed with details, examples, and discussions. |
| **Information Literacy:** demonstrates ability to use college-level academic research to develop complex ideas significantly. | **Information Literacy:** demonstrates ability to use college-level academic research to develop ideas. | **Information Literacy:** demonstrates ability to use relevant college-level academic research to discuss topic. | **Information Literacy:** weak research and information literacy ability: very few sources, little variety of sources, and little obvious effort to conduct scholarly/professional research. |
| **Sources:** introduced and integrated to advance essay's purpose and meet audience expectations. | **Sources:** introduced and integrated in ways that meet the essay's goals and purposes. | **Sources:** included within the general requirements of an applicable style guide. | **Sources:** language and materials from sources presented is hard-to-follow; unintentional, careless misuse of source material would be plagiarism if intentional; sources do not support and might contradict writer's views attributed to them. |

## ORGANIZATION

| A Paper Characteristics | B Paper Characteristics | C Paper Characteristics | D Paper Characteristics |
|---|---|---|---|
| **Title and Introduction:** appropriately informs reader of topic, purpose, and focus; motivates audience to read. | **Title and Introduction:** well-chosen, appropriate to topic and focus. | **Title and Introduction:** generally match topic and focus. | **Title and Introduction:** missing, misleading, or overly general. |
| **Paragraphs:** organized purposefully and developed substantially with evidence, examples, and reasoning. | **Paragraphs:** organized clearly and developed adequately with evidence, examples, and reasoning; some paragraphs may lack richness of detail or evidence. | **Paragraphs:** make sense, points usually supported with some evidence or detailed examples. | **Paragraphs:** frequently unrelated to each other or repetitive; don't develop logically from start to finish, or break in illogical places; often end without developing broad, general statements with evidence and reasoning. |
| **Paragraphing:** contributes to greater understanding of the whole. | **Paragraphing:** information broken into parts that make sense, assist effective reading. | **Paragraphing:** generally establishes overall organizational pattern for readers to follow. | **Paragraphing:** shows a weak organization pattern; can be difficult to understand how one paragraph is connected to the next. |
| **Order of Discussion:** paper guides reader in explicit, clear, and purposeful ways (including transitions when necessary). | **Order of Discussion:** focus is identifiable and can be followed through entire discussion; transitions between and within paragraphs advance writer's ideas. | **Order of Discussion:** develops basic focus, with few paragraphs out of sequence or off track; transitions from one section/idea to another are evident and make sense. | **Order of Discussion:** focus is not readily apparent; transitions between and within paragraphs are weak, ineffective, or misleading. |
| **Order of Information:** ordered in a meaningful pattern; order of information clearly supports focus and purpose. | **Order of Information:** focus and purpose are identifiable by order in which information appears; overall patterns make sense. | **Order of Information:** some patterns make sense, though the overall focus may be unclear. | **Order of Information:** does not establish clear patterns for readers to follow. |
| **Conclusion:** satisfying sense that purpose has been achieved. | **Conclusion:** gives sense that the discussion ends at a good place. | **Conclusion:** may summarize the ideas in the essay but does not explain why ideas are significant. | **Conclusion:** essay ends abruptly and without resolution. |

## STYLE

| A Paper Characteristics | B Paper Characteristics | C Paper Characteristics | D Paper Characteristics |
|---|---|---|---|
| **Word choice**: precise, interesting, appropriate to writing purpose and audience. | **Word choice**: generally appropriate to writing purpose and audience. | **Word choice**: most words well-chosen and fit purpose and audience. | **Word choice**: poor word choices make reading difficult. |
| **Language**: mature, purposefully controlled. | **Language**: generally mature and purposefully controlled. | **Language**: somewhat mature and controlled. | **Language**: uncontrolled use of language; simplistic vocabulary throughout. |
| **Sentences**: often active statements; uses efficient and effective modification. | **Sentences**: typically active statements, extended by efficient and effective modification. | **Sentences**: generally readable and make sense; sometimes feature efficient and effective modifying clauses/phrases. | **Sentences**: disordered sentence parts, poor phrasing; make reading difficult; often disregard normal rules of standard written English in ways that make ideas hard to understand. |
| **Sentence Structure**: varies according to content, purpose, and audience. | **Sentence Structure**: varies in structure, only occasionally is choppy, rambling, or repetitive. | **Sentence Structure**: sentences are occasionally choppy, long and rambling, vague and wordy, or repetitive. | **Sentence Structure**: often short and choppy, long and rambling, vague and wordy, or repetitive. |
| **Voice**: consistent, complements purpose, fits the genre, and appeals to audience. | **Voice**: consistent and appropriate for genre, purpose, and audience. | **Voice**: consistent and appropriate, usually fitting genre, purpose, and audience. | **Voice**: often inappropriate for genre, purpose, and audience. |
| **Sources**: information and quotes integrated skillfully into writer's own sentences and paragraphs. | **Sources**: information and quotes make sense within writer's own sentences and paragraphs. | **Sources**: information and quotes clearly presented as source material. | **Sources**: information and quotes dropped into paragraphs without context or transitions. |

## MECHANICS

| A Paper Characteristics | B Paper Characteristics | C Paper Characteristics | D Paper Characteristics |
| --- | --- | --- | --- |
| **Format:** consistent with MLA, APA, or other style guide. | **Format:** appropriate, generally follows MLA, APA, or other style guide. | **Format:** generally appropriate for the purpose, usually follows MLA, APA, or other style guide. | **Format:** careless attention to basic requirements of applicable style guides (including use of graphics). |
| **References:** cited and documented according to appropriate style guide so quoted sources are easily identified. | **References:** cited and documented according to appropriate style guide so it can be determined when sources have been used and can be found. | **References:** generally cited and documented, if not always appropriately; reader can determine when sources are quoted or referenced; instances of unreferenced sources are few and clearly not intentional. | **References:** language or material not cited clearly; documentation is generally wrong according to assigned style guide, often in ways that interfere with reader's ability to find source material and locate referenced portions; shows careless attention to important requirements for quoting, paraphrasing, and citing, raising questions of possible plagiarism. |
| **Grammar, Spelling, Punctuation:** do not interfere with communication. | **Grammar, Spelling, Punctuation:** mistakes rarely interfere with communication. | **Grammar, Spelling, Punctuation:** mistakes sometimes interfere with writer's credibility or reader's ability to read easily. | **Grammar, Spelling, Punctuation:** many errors in spelling, grammar, punctuation, word choice, and usage make reading difficult or limit writer's credibility. |
| **Editing:** effectively shows attention to audience's desire to read without interruption from unexpected errors. | **Editing:** usually shows attention to audience's desire to read without interruption from unexpected errors. | **Editing:** shows some attention to reader's desire to read without interruption from unexpected errors. | **Editing:** does not show attention to reader's desire to read without interruption from unexpected errors. |

# GRADING IN FIRST-YEAR WRITING

## PORTFOLIO SUBMISSION GUIDELINES

Your portfolio is due by the end of the last class before finals week, unless your instructor's syllabus sets a different deadline. Electronic portfolios will be prepared and submitted according to instructions that you will receive in class and that are found on the Department of Writing portfolio site (https://www.gvsu.edu/writing/portfolio). If your portfolio is late, you may fail the course.

Your final portfolio will consist of three final papers. The following instructions apply unless your instructor gives you other special instructions:

▶ Margins should be one inch all the way around the page.
▶ All lines should be double-spaced.
▶ Fonts should be common or default types (e.g., Arial, Calibri, Times New Roman), and the point-size should be 11 or 12.

If your instructor has special instructions for the form or format of your papers, the portfolio grading groups will honor those instructions.

In addition to requiring you to submit earlier drafts, your instructor is entitled to set further requirements before your portfolio will be eligible for grading. Common requirements are that you submit papers on time in response to individual assignments, submit substantial revisions, use particular formats, or submit papers at a specific length or level of editing care. If you do not meet your instructor's specific requirements, your instructor may refuse to submit your portfolio for grading, in which case you will fail the course. Such requirements will be set out clearly in your instructor's syllabus, assignments, or other written instructions, and if you have questions about those requirements, you should ask your instructor.

Instructors do not comment on portfolios, so your portfolio will not be returned to you. You should keep copies of your work and wait for grade reports to see your course grades. The Department of Writing may keep your portfolio and use it for studies of our teaching and its results, but we will not publish the contents of your writing or share it with future classes without your permission.

## PORTFOLIO GRADING

We determine all final grades in WRT 130 and WRT 150 by having a group of instructors read and evaluate your final portfolio. Your instructor has been placed in a portfolio group this semester, and this group will grade your portfolio. We use this method so that our grading can be as fair and accurate as possible. Our instructors work very hard to make sure that this method gives you the fairest result.

Over the course of the semester your instructor's portfolio grading group (usually four to six instructors) reads and discusses samples of writing from their classes throughout the semester to agree about standards for A, B, C, and D papers. Their standards begin with those established by the Department of Writing and explained more specifically earlier in the Guide. Through their discussions, the groups work to fit those standards more specifically to your assignments and the work done by your class.

At the end of the semester, your instructor and one other instructor from the portfolio grading group will read and grade your portfolio using whole letter grades. If they disagree about the grade, a third instructor in that group reads your portfolio to decide which reader, your instructor or the other instructor, has come closest to the standards that the portfolio group has agreed upon during the semester. For example, if your portfolio receives a B from the first two readers, you receive a B on your portfolio. If your portfolio receives an A from one reader, a B from another, and an A from a third reader, you receive an A on your portfolio. By using this method, we seek to arrive at a "community" grade based on the quality of your writing rather than a grade based solely on one instructor's preferences or on your instructor's personal opinion of you.

Once the portfolio grading group arrives at a letter grade, your instructor also has the option of adding a "plus" or "minus" to the final letter grade based on other aspects of your work, such as attendance, class participation, effective peer review, and completion of reading assignments. Instructors should not raise or lower your grade any further than a plus or minus, which ensures the highest degree of fairness based on the quality of your work.

The portfolios are graded after class is over, so the portfolios are not returned. For those reasons, we do not write comments on the papers in the portfolios. Instructors do often write very brief notes about grades of D, so students earning this grade may ask about the reasons for that grade.

If you have any questions about the grade that you receive, ask your instructor to discuss your grade with you.

## SEMESTER-LONG EVALUATION

The fact that you earn your grade with your final portfolio does not mean that the evaluation of your writing should be a mystery. First, you should learn how to apply the grading criteria to your own writing. Your instructor will read your writing throughout the semester and respond to it with comments and suggestions for revision. Many instructors will have you read, comment on, and evaluate other students' work. For most students, a grade is not necessary for early drafts because the proper focus is on what the paper could become, not on what it is. But if you want a grade on an assignment and your instructor has not given one, just ask. Instructors will be able to tell you where they think the paper falls within the range of A to D. Your instructor will probably tell you what the portfolio group has been saying about writing like yours.

Nevertheless, it is important to remember that all grade estimates—whether they are by you, your instructor, or your classmates—are just that: estimates. Ultimately, the grade will depend

> "Take this course seriously. When papers are assigned to you, start right away. Use all the help you can get to make your papers the best."
> —Jacob R.

on the entire portfolio in its final form, something nobody will be able to review carefully until the end of the term. Mainly what you need to do is just keep on working. If the instructor says your paper is probably a low B or a C, your next question should be: "What could I work on in this paper that would improve it?" Improve your work until the very last day, and you will receive the best grade available to you. Meanwhile, you should also seek to improve your own judgment of your own grade, using the grading criteria. The most successful and satisfied students do not need the instructor to tell them what grade they are getting; they already have a good idea themselves.

## MIDTERM EVALUATION

Grand Valley requires midterm grade reports for first-year students and some upper-level students. Midterm grades are available on the Web but not recorded on your official transcript. Midterm grades in WRT 130 and WRT 150 can only assess the overall quality of your work in the class up to that point and your prospects for doing better. Such assessments have no direct bearing on your final grade. For a full explanation of your midterm grade, please consult with your instructor.

## GRADE APPEALS

If for any reason you need to appeal your final grade, please consult the Student Code for the applicable procedures. Your first contact should be with the instructor of your class. Appeals from your instructor's decision to the Department of Writing should be supported by a written appeal explaining how your portfolio displays the characteristics of the grade that you are seeking. Your written appeal itself should display most characteristics of the grade that you seek. Appeals to the Director of First-Year Writing may be forwarded by e-mail at wrtdept@gvsu.edu or delivered to the Department of Writing directed to the attention of the Director of First-Year Writing.

# PORTFOLIO GRADING FAQ: QUESTIONS YOU MIGHT HAVE

1.  **Why is a group of first-year writing instructors reading my papers and determining my final grade rather than just my own instructor?**

A group of four to six instructors (including your instructor) has been reading samples of your class's writing throughout the semester to discuss and agree about what is an A, B, C, D, and F portfolio. The goal of the instructors in the group is to set fair and accurate grading standards. The standards will develop after discussing samples from your class and other classes throughout the semester. This carefully considered agreement between two writing instructors results in more consistent and fair grades than any other method.

2.  **Does my instructor have any say as to what grade I get on my portfolio and what grade I receive in this class?**

Yes. Your instructor will always be one of at least two portfolio readers of your work at the end of the term. If the second reader in the group agrees with your instructor about the grade for your portfolio, then that agreement will determine the grade you receive on the portfolio. If the second reader does not agree with your instructor, then a third reader will be asked to read your portfolio. If the third reader agrees with your instructor, then the grade stands. If the third reader agrees with the second reader, then your grade is based on the agreement of readers two and three. The goal is to arrive at a community grade rather than a grade based solely on one instructor's preferences.

3.  **What happens if one person in the portfolio group grades much harder than the others? Doesn't this mean I'll probably get a low grade if that person reads my portfolio?**

No, not necessarily. If the second reader does not agree with your instructor, a third reader is asked to read your portfolio and decide which of the first two readers is closest to the standards that the portfolio group has agreed about during the semester. (See question #2.) The portfolio groups also work to discourage instructors from being "hard" or "easy." We strive to have all instructors arrive at a common understanding of what portfolios deserve which grades, grounding their judgment in our detailed grading descriptions.

**4.  Shouldn't each instructor grade his or her own students' work?**

All instructors have a hand in grading their own students' work, but the portfolio groups assure students that their grades are a reflection of community standards—departmental and university-wide.

**5.  How can the portfolio group grade my papers if they haven't seen the assignment?**

WRT 130 and WRT 150 are courses designed to give you practice and instruction in the various kinds of writing that you will be asked to do throughout college. All instructors design their assignments with that goal in mind. The portfolio group, therefore, wants to be general in their assessment of your writing. They want to look at three samples of your writing and describe the group of three as "excellent," "good," "average," or "below average or failing." The ideal is that this grade reflects what most professors would say if they picked up your portfolio and read it. We want your grade to be based on the general quality of your writing alone, not on how well the writing satisfies instructor-specific instructions.

**6.  My instructor said that I have to type single-space, have fewer than two sentence fragments, and underline the thesis statement in every essay just to get a C. If the portfolio group doesn't know this, then what happens?**

Instructors often have minimum requirements that they want every paper to meet. For example, some say that a paper can't be handed in more than one day late. When instructors have such requirements that may not be the same as other instructors in the portfolio group, they will enforce those requirements by making sure you meet them before you submit a portfolio to the portfolio group at the end of the term. This way, everyone who reads your portfolio will assume it has met any instructor-specific minimum requirements. If you don't meet minimum requirements that your instructor sets, your instructor won't allow you to submit a portfolio at the end of the term.

7. **Could two people in my portfolio group agree that I deserve a B and then my instructor give me a C anyway because of absences or class participation?**

That should not happen. The portfolio grade is your letter grade for the semester. Typically you should not expect your grade to be adjusted—either up or down—by your instructor beyond a plus or a minus for the letter grade the portfolio group gives you. If your grade needs adjusting down, you probably didn't meet the minimum requirements (e.g., too many absences) and you should not have been allowed to submit a portfolio in the first place, meaning you would deserve an F. If an instructor over in Biology looks up your grade in WRT 130 or WRT 150, they should be assured that this grade basically reflects how well you write, not your attendance, your improvement, or your good (or bad) attitude—as should also be true in your Biology class.

8. **Just looking at my portfolio at the end of the term doesn't show how much I've improved. Shouldn't my grade be based, at least in part, on my improvement?**

We do not believe it makes sense to grade on improvement itself. Your grade in WRT 130 or WRT 150 should be based on the quality of your writing at the end of the term. This way, what counts as A, B, C, D, or F is the same for every student, or at least as close to being the same as we can manage. Instructors can adjust grades (usually with a plus or a minus) based on your participation, improvement, or other factors. "Improvement" itself is probably impossible to measure accurately even if we wished to do so. We hope that your improvement will earn its proper reward when we decide how well you are writing by the end of the term when you submit your portfolio.

9. **I like to have grades during the semester so that I know how well I am doing. I don't want my grade at the end of the term to come as a big surprise.**

We agree that you should know how you are doing, but we do not believe interim grades would be the most effective approach to that need. Your instructor will be reading your writing throughout the semester and responding to it with comments, personal conferences, personal conferences, endnotes, and suggestions for revision. Most first-year writing classes have consultants from the Writing Center that work with you and point out strengths and weaknesses in your writing. And many instructors will have you read and comment on other students' work. For most students, a grade is not necessary for early drafts because the proper focus is on what the paper could be, not on what it is. But if you want a grade on an assignment and your instructor has not given one, just ask. The professor will be able to tell you where she thinks the paper falls within the range of A to F. The instructor will probably tell you what she and others in the portfolio group have been saying about writing like yours. Don't be surprised if the instructor says, for example, that some in the group might say C and she, or others in the group, might say B. Group members often disagree, especially early in the semester, about what is an A, B, C, or D. If your professor says your paper is probably a low B or a C, your next question should be: "What could I work on in this paper that would improve it?" Your instructor should love this question and this should give you the feedback you need to feel encouraged to try making even a good paper better. In the end, if you simply do the best you can with a reasonable amount of hard work, your grade at the end will be the best that you can earn. The last thing any of us would want to do is to encourage students to stop working before they have achieved the best work they can manage.

**10. It seems to me that the portfolio-grading system is all about judging final products. Aren't we supposed to be interested in the writing process?**

Our first-year writing program does stress learning strategies and skills that help you develop your own writing process. In fact, because the portfolio group grading system focuses on what you can do at the end of the semester, it encourages and gives opportunity for every paper to be revised. Revision is the heart of the writing process. That is, we teach and value better writing processes because they do tend to produce better writing. In the end, we believe that grading your results keeps the best focus on learning to use writing processes effectively.

## 11. What is supposed to be in my portfolio?

Every student should submit three papers, including at least one with citations and references, that show your ability to conduct scholarly research and use its results effectively. Ask your instructor if you are not sure. Your instructor and the other students should help you make good choices about what goes in the final portfolio.

## 12. Can I include a paper in my portfolio from another class?

You should not plan to include an essay written in another class in your final portfolio unless you receive permission from the instructors of both classes and make arrangements with your writing instructor about what you can use and how you can use it. Without earlier arrangements like that, all papers in your portfolio must have been assigned and seen by your instructor, and they must be originally created for the class you are taking. Students who secretly submit work from another class (even an earlier first-year writing class) violate the Student Code's provisions on academic honesty and integrity, a very serious matter. The results may include failing the course and being reported to the Dean of Students for further action.

The only exception to this rule would be for students in WRT 130; if you are a WRT 130 student, it is perfectly acceptable (and even encouraged) for you to include a paper you began in WRT 120 last semester in the final portfolio you submit in WRT 130. If you do submit work in your final WRT 130 portfolio that you began in WRT 120, you should expect to make significant revisions to the essay before turning it in.

# RESOURCES FOR STUDENT WRITERS AT GRAND VALLEY

## LIBRARY RESOURCES

The goal of library-related instruction in first-year writing classes is to help you become a lifelong learner who can use your information literacy skills to conduct academic and professional research and integrate your findings into your writing accurately, ethically, and effectively. In order to reach this goal, you will learn how to develop and implement a research strategy, locate the resources necessary to meet your information needs, and evaluate the information that you find.

Many writing instructors work closely with Grand Valley librarians and bring librarians into class to help you learn how to use Grand Valley's libraries and online library resources. In addition, each class has a designated library liaison who will work with you on your research for your essays. Ask your instructor for the name of your library liaison, or feel free to ask library staff to help you find the right person. Grand Valley librarians are eager and ready to help you search for and select the best sources for your paper, develop research questions, identify research strategies, evaluate the usefulness of specific sources, and find relevant and reliable information online. Library liaisons are available in person, by e-mail, or by telephone. We encourage you to ask for their help.

Peer research consultants are also available to help you get started using the library's collection to write your paper. They are students themselves and are highly trained in sharing information literacy skills. The library's research consultants work alongside writing consultants and speech consultants in the Knowledge Market, which you can find in the Grand Valley libraries in Allendale and Grand Rapids. For more information or to schedule an appointment visit www.gvsu.edu/library/km.

## COMPUTER CLASSROOMS

Your first-year writing class will typically meet in a computer classroom once a week and in a traditional classroom on the other day or days your class is scheduled to meet. Computer classrooms are sometimes used simply for writing and revising drafts, but your instructor may introduce a range of activities—brief in-class writing exercises, peer review sessions, and research assignments, for example—to help you gain expertise in a range of writing skills and strategies.

Any Grand Valley computer that you use in a computer classroom gives you the option to save items to a personal drive (the "N" drive), or cloud drives (OneDrive or Google Drive). You can access items saved to your network account from various campus locations, such as other campus computer labs and some campus living quarters, as well as from other Grand Valley campuses. You can also retrieve items on the N drive from an off-campus home computer. You have access to your cloud drives through any device that has an Internet connection on campus and off. Seek assistance from Grand Valley's IT office (616-331-2101) for more information about saving files.

The computer classrooms use recent versions of Microsoft Word for Windows as the primary word processing software. This means that Microsoft Works documents, Apple Pages documents, and other documents do not open in a computer classroom unless you have saved them in a compatible format like rich-text format (.rtf), which you can do with nearly any word processing program. It also means that documents prepared in the computer classroom will not open on some other computers, especially older computers, unless you have saved them in rich-text format or another format used on that computer. Your instructor may be able to suggest other programs and methods for working on the same files both at home and in a computer classroom.

# THE FRED MEIJER CENTER FOR WRITING

Peer writing consultants work in all of the writing center locations as well as in WRT 130 and WRT 150 classes. Consultants provide helpful feedback, offer advice, model writing strategies, and ask questions in order to help students improve as writers. Consultants do not simply check grammar and mechanics, nor do they predict what grade a paper may receive. Essentially, the role of a consultant is to provide a well-trained pair of eyes to help writers think more critically about their own writing, provide reader feedback, and to assist writers in devising a plan for revision.

> *"Talk to the writing consultants, ask your professor questions... They want you to be successful. Utilize them."*
> —*Bernadette J.*

Most instructors use computer classrooms for consultations. In that setting, students have instant access to a consultant who can discuss any issue that may arise while you are working through writing activities or drafting and revising your papers. For example, you might need a quick discussion about the purpose of topic sentences, a guided tour through the library's many online resources for research, or a more in-depth conference about a whole draft. Make a point to seek out your writing consultant often. When you establish a working relationship with your writing consultant, they will come to understand your unique writing strengths and challenges, and can offer useful advice that is designed to help you with your current and future writing projects.

Consultants also will lead small-group discussions in first-year writing classes. Small groups serve as a place to cultivate ideas, expand and clarify key elements, and devise a plan for a paper. The consultant's role in these situations is to help the group stay on track, encourage everyone's involvement in the discussion, model or prompt the group to use effective feedback strategies, and offer another perspective on your writing.

Here are some tips for making your group discussions work:

► Come prepared with specific questions or areas of your writing for which you need feedback.

► Bring enough copies of your draft for each student and the consultant to have one. This allows your readers to follow along and write comments on the papers, which you might find helpful later in your revision process.

> ► Solicit the advice of everyone in your group, not just the writing consultant. The more reader input you have, the better sense you have about how readers understand your ideas.

In labs or small-group discussions, consultants are there as a resource to work through your individual writing needs. Get to know your classroom consultants early in the semester, and consider visiting them outside of class, when they are on duty in the writing center (LOH 120) or at any of the other Fred Meijer Center for Writing locations, including the Allendale Knowledge Market (Mary Idema Pew Library), the Steelcase Knowledge Market (Steelcase Library—DeVos–Pew campus), and online through Google Docs. For a list of all available locations and services, as well as writing resources and how-to guides, please visit the writing center Web site: gvsu.edu/wc.

# EXEMPLARY FIRST-YEAR WRITING PORTFOLIOS

When we set out to choose student writing to be published in this textbook, we don't try to anticipate which ones will serve as perfect models for future students. Instead, our goal is to select writers who understand their paper's purposes and seek to challenge themselves with complex, interesting, and timely topics. We look for writers who know what they are trying to accomplish in their work, and authors who keep their audience in mind as they write. We also wanted to offer you a range of styles, subjects, and assignments, so that you can see the variety of approaches students take to successfully accomplish their writing goals.

No matter what your assignment may be, the keys to good writing remain consistent—a solid sense of purpose, focus, and audience. In showcasing work from previous first-year writing students, we hope to open up classroom dialogue about the content as well as the writing. We have chosen twelve writers to showcase in this year's edition of the book, and each has something special to offer.

Before each student's writing, you'll find a brief description of the essays included, as well as an explanation of why the *Guide's* editors selected the portfolio—the strengths we saw and admired in each student's work. You'll also find reflections from the writers about their experiences as a first-year writing student. They offer sound advice about strategies you might consider trying as a student writer this semester.

# PORTFOLIO ONE

## BY MICHAEL FARWIG

For Michael Farwig, who recently graduated from Grand Valley with a degree in Public Administration, Professor Jim Van Sickle's class gave him a chance to explore topics that he found interesting and engaging. As he says, "I went to class to read about baseball for my argumentative essay. How cool is that?"

Michael's first essay, "Playing with Fireworks: The Epidemic of PTSD in Today's Veterans" builds on his experience as a soldier, exploring the epidemic of PTSD and its effects on US military veterans. When you read his second essay, "A Case for a Clean Cooperstown" you'll see how Michael's love of baseball informed his argument about the influence of performance-enhancing drugs on the Baseball Hall of Fame. Michael is most proud of this essay, because he was "able to make an argument and defend it . . . in my voice instead of a rigid academic style." Michael's final essay, "Two Tuesdays in Kandahar: My Forty-Eight Hours in a Never-Ending War," describes the mental and physical challenge of his military deployment in Kandahar, Afghanistan, examining the complicated experiences of a soldier's life.

Michael's portfolio illustrates the value of using personal experience as a starting point for research and writing. Although you might not have experiences as dramatic as Michael's, we encourage you to use your interests, passions, curiosity, and life experiences to generate ideas that you can explore through writing.

### Michael's Advice for First-Year Writing Students

Utilize every resource you have. The library has great research tools and people to help you use them, the writing center's workers know how to put together an essay, and your professors want to see you succeed and will help you if you ask. Use all of them and write about what you love and you can't fail.

# PLAYING WITH FIREWORKS:
# THE EPIDEMIC OF PTSD IN TODAY'S VETERANS

The firework explodes without warning, and I can hear the war again. Afghanistan is seven thousand miles away and five years in the past, but with each blast in the sky, I am drawn back. The first boom rings out, and I can hear the grenades striking outside my tent. It fizzles in the sky, sending sparkles showering down, and brings with it the medevac helicopters beating rotors and the stuttering fire of AK-47s. The second detonation is the IED blast under my vehicle, the one that sent me to the hospital. Another and another and another, the flashes light the sky, and my mind is filled with the horrors of my war. Firework shows, a scene of jubilance and joy, are often a nightmare for a returning veteran like me with post-traumatic stress disorder (PTSD). This disorder has been around under different names and diagnoses since at least the Civil War and has had different recognized symptoms and triggers. While PTSD can be present in anyone, it is especially prevalent in the veteran community because of the trauma they face. This growing epidemic amongst veterans, caused by nearly two decades of a new kind of war, has already had dramatic effects. As of 2015, there had been 2.7 million Americans deployed to Iraq or Afghanistan ("US Veterans & Military Families") and it is estimated that nearly twenty three percent of those veterans suffer from PTSD (Fulton et al. 99). Many of these returning heroes struggle with reintegrating to society, dealing with numerous medical, social, and psychological challenges the average citizen doesn't know or understand. Those in the mental health community are developing a number of treatment options to combat the growing need, although the very nature of the disorder has presented great difficulty in finding an effective "cure," and while we continue to attempt to even define the disease, the effects ravage those afflicted. Post-traumatic stress disorder is a misunderstood and often overlooked mental health crisis. Its occurrence is growing amongst returning veterans due to the new style of warfare and currently there are limited effective treatments and a number of barriers to care, causing severe problems with rehabilitation and returning to normalcy.

PTSD is not necessarily a new phenomenon; rather, it has been around under different guises in every war in history, dating back to the Greeks. However, understanding of the illness has dramatically evolved, and veterans are seeing a greater occurrence in recent conflicts. Walter McDermott, an author on PTSD and a Vietnam veteran, states that it was first recognized in modern warfare as a soldier's illness in the Civil War, where a physician, Dr. Mendez De Costa, noticed what is now known to be a symptom of PTSD, a racing heart. He attributed this to a cardiovascular disorder he named *Soldier's Heart*. He names off the various other titles it has gone under in each of the following wars: *Shellshock* in World War 1, *Combat Fatigue* in World War II, *Post-Vietnam Syndrome* in Vietnam (McDermott 7). The name changes reflected a progressing understanding of the illness in soldiers. Mental health professionals no longer considers the disorder to be a mental exhaustion and prescribe simple bed rest as they did with World War II veterans (7). Now there are a number of different therapies and medications targeted at treating the psychological trauma. However, even now there is a debate over what to call the illness and how to treat it: "Post Traumatic Stress Disorder," "Combat Stress," "Post Traumatic Stress Syndrome," all appear on my military and veteran's medical records, with prescribed treatments ranging from talk therapy to a daily intensive reliance on prescription medication. The distressing part is that it is clear that PTSD has been around since the beginning of warfare but it is occurring at a higher rate in recent conflicts than those of wars past.

There are many reasons that today's veterans are experiencing increased rates of PTSD, but there are two chief amongst them: the style of conflict, and the signature wounds of these wars. Today's soldiers, while possibly having a decreased intensity of combat, are seeing it a much higher rate. According to a Vietnam history website: "The average infantryman in the South Pacific during World War II saw about 40 days of combat in four years. The average infantryman in Vietnam saw about 240 days of combat ("Vietnam War Facts, Stats and Myths"). It is also not just the infantryman who is fighting today's wars. Whereas in the past, a transportation soldier or human resources specialist wouldn't be anywhere near the frontlines, that is no longer the case. A cook in my unit in Afghanistan was awarded the Purple Heart and Bronze Star with Valor for his actions during a firefight at our outpost. Today's support specialists are consistently placed in danger because there are no longer enemy lines; the war is now everywhere. This prolonged, drawn-out nature of conflict and the increasing number of participants are contributors to the rise in PTSD.

Today's soldiers are not only seeing increased rates of combat, but the types of wounds inflicted are directly linked to post-traumatic stress. The survival rate of OIF/OEF is almost 90% with a rate of nearly 15-1 wounded to killed ratio (Kinney 22). This means more soldiers are surviving but are often coming home with devastating injuries. Couple that with the fact that the signature injury they are receiving is directly linked to PTSD, and there is a recipe for an epidemic. The primary weapon in the Afghanistan and Iraq wars is the improvised explosive device (IED). The explosive force of this blast damages the internal organs even more often than it proves fatal. In the case of the brain, it creates a severe concussion-like wound known as traumatic brain injury (TBI). Many of the symptoms of TBI are similar to those of PTSD, and TBIs are directly correlated to an increased risk of PTSD. *The Diagnostic and Statistical Manual of Mental Disorders: 5th edition* (DSM V), places comorbidity at 48% between the two disorders (Diagnostic 280). So not only are soldiers being wounded at a higher rate, the very wounds themselves are causing psychological trauma. This increased number of soldiers with PTSD has brought new awareness and understanding of the disorder.

One of the ways the mental health community is changing the understanding of this disorder is attempting to provide a clearer definition of what PTSD is and how it affects people. In 2013, the American Psychiatry Association released its updated book of mental health disorders, with new diagnostic standards and statistics on post-traumatic stress. The *DSM V*, considered to be the bible of psychiatric diagnoses, has given eight specific criteria for diagnosing post-traumatic stress ranging from flashbacks and trouble sleeping, to anxiety, depression, and increased anger (Diagnostic 271-72). The *DSM V* estimates that only 3.5% of adults have a twelve-month prevalence of PTSD but that the rates amongst veterans are higher, with the highest rates amongst combat survivors (276). This startling statistic shows that the effects of combat are directly linked to this psychological disorder. The consequences of these combined symptoms are devastating, with the *DSM V* noting that veterans with this disorder have huge functional impairments causing lower income, lower education, and reduced relationship in society and family (278–79).

This impaired functioning makes returning and reintegrating from war a tremendously difficult task for veterans suffering from this illness. Even those veterans without a PTSD diagnosis struggle with coming home and adapting to civilian life, but PTSD makes the problem significantly more difficult. Nina Sayer, the Deputy Director for the Center for Chronic Disease Outcomes Research and Research Director for Polytrauma and Blast-Related Injuries for the VA, found in her study that "nearly all (96 percent) of a group of post-9/11 combat veterans surveyed reported that they were interested in receiving services to ease 'community reintegration problems'" (Sayer et al. 589). She goes on to note that "More than one-half of this select population was struggling with anger control problems, and nearly one-third had engaged in behaviors that put themselves or others at risk since homecoming" and that the problem was increased in the population of veterans with PTSD (Sayer et al. 594). This reintegration problem is increased because of the many symptoms of PTSD and the functional impairment it can cause. Having increased rates of homelessness, unemployability, and increased relationship stress cause significant stressors to those returning home. An article done by Tori DeAngelis for the American Psychological Association found that two thirds of homeless Operation Iraqi/Enduring Freedom had PTSD (DeAngelis). Oftentimes, veterans feel unanchored to the civilian society, feeling adrift from their peers' social circles. PTSD only increases these issues. Unfortunately, a number of times they are unable to cope at all. *The New York Times* reports that as of 2016, the suicide rate of veterans had risen 35% (Philipps). A VA study on suicide suggested that as many as twenty veterans a day take their own lives (United States). That same data report stated that the number of veterans committing suicide makes up eighteen percent of all suicides in the US (United States). Coming home from multiple deployments, only to take one's life because of a war-caused mental illness isn't just a heartbreaking tragedy played out in movies and novels, it is too often the reality for our heroes. These frightening statistics show the need for increased mental health options for veterans.

These options for treatment are beginning to become a much bigger priority due to the increasing demand, with there being two main approaches to rehabilitation: psychotherapy, and pharmacology. Miriam Reisman, an author of a report on effectiveness of PTSD treatments, states that psychotherapy is the "first-line" in

PTSD treatment. She explains that the two most effective types of psychotherapy are cognitive behavioral therapy and prolonged exposure therapy (Reisman 625). Cognitive behavioral therapy attempts to change the way a person thinks, using talk therapy to alter negative thoughts and feelings. Prolonged exposure is similar, but it focuses specifically on the trauma and trying to explain the anxieties it causes and how to overcome them (Reisman 625). Reisman notes that prolonged exposure has been shown to be effective in sixty percent of veterans with PTSD (Reisman 625). While that appears to be a welcome number, it means that forty percent of veterans are left dealing with symptoms. This failure is why new therapies are still being developed to combat PTSD; chief among them is eye movement desensitization and reprocessing, or EMDR. The EMDR institute explains EMDR process: the patient retells the trauma to a trained psychiatrist while focusing on a moving object such as the psychiatrists finger in the hope that this will make the patient remember trauma without the emotional stress. ("What is EMDR?"). The effectiveness of this new style of treatment is still being studied, but it does appear to be promising. A number of other therapy types are being developed, as well as alternative and holistic approaches but cognitive behavioral therapy remains the standard treatment plan.

These cognitive behavioral therapies are most often combined with the pharmacology approach. Walter Alexander, who writes for the National Institute of Health, writes that the FDA has approved only two drugs for the treatment of PTSD: sertraline (Zoloft) and paroxetine HCl (Paxil). He explains that these are selective serotonin reuptake inhibitors; they work affecting serotonin levels which regulate "mood, anxiety, appetite, sleep, and other bodily functions." Alexander states that eighty-nine percent of veterans diagnosed with PTSD are treated with these medications (Alexander 32). Eighty nine percent is a tremendously large number, especially since there are those that argue that some drugs are ineffective for treatment in PTSD. Whitney McKnight, a writer for *Clinical Psychiatry News*, writes that Veteran's Affairs and Department of Defense are changing their guidelines of care to recommend therapy over medication. She cites the new guidelines as specifically recommending against specific medications (McKnight). It is alarming that some of the medications that are explicitly recommended against, soldiers I have served with and I have been prescribed, even after the guideline's release in 2013. The VA is not following its own procedures in treating those afflicted, possibly causing more harm than good.

These treatments, though an improvement over the past, still come with numerous problems and obstacles. One of the first obstacles that must be overcome is the stigma within the military. Soldiers are used to hearing "drive on." It is a cultural joke that even a gunshot wound can be treated with Tylenol and water. This attitude often perceives seeking care to be a sign of weakness, and that perception is only magnified when discussing mental health. The Committee on the Assessment of the Readjustment Needs of Military Personnel, found that thirty-seven percent of military members in a study on PTSD had a stigma-related reason as a barrier to care (Committee et al. 91). This is a tough mindset to leave behind, even after exiting the military, but those that are able still face other challenges. The VA is under a tremendous burden from the influx of returning veterans, and has been unable to keep up with the rising demand for care. A recent *USA Today* report stated that "the inspector general looked at primary and mental health care appointments for new patients and referrals for specialists and found that overall, 36% had to wait longer than a month for an appointment" (Slack). Combine these long waits with the fact that the treatments provided still haven't shown much continued success in treating prolonged PTSD, and many veterans avoid seeking care altogether. In fact, "Only about 60% of returning Veterans are engaged in VA care" (Averill et al. 1), and that is all VA care, not just mental health. With so many roadblocks in place to mental health care, it is no wonder that this illness is affecting more veterans than ever.

Post-traumatic stress disorder is reaching epidemic levels amongst the veteran population. As the war against terror drags on in Afghanistan and because of the very nature of the war they fight, more veterans will come home with this terrible illness than ever before. These veterans will continue to struggle to return to civilian society, and some will continue to take their own lives. The mental health community is trying to develop treatments and medications to fight against PTSD, in large part due to the light the veteran population has shined on it, but these have not proven effective. But while there are still significant barriers to overcome in getting help and the therapies used, the veteran community is ready to face these challenges head on just as they faced the battles they fought in. The fireworks are exploding again, and they can hear the war still in them. Their hearts may still race, but hopefully soon they can join the crowd in their awe and happiness. Hopefully soon they can rejoin society and finally come home.

*Word Count: 2485*

## Works Cited

Alexander, Walter. "Pharmacotherapy for Post-Traumatic Stress Disorder In Combat Veterans: Focus on Antidepressants and Atypical Antipsychotic Agents." *Pharmacy and Therapeutics,* Vol.37, No.1 (2012): 32–38. Accessed 27 Jan. 2018.

Averill, Lynnette A. et al. "Research on PTSD Prevalence in OEF/OIF Veterans: Expanding Investigation of Demographic Variables." *European Journal of Psychotraumatology* Vol. 6 (2015), 1–5: doi10.3402/ejpt.v6.27322. *PMC.* 10 Apr. 2018.

Committee on the Assessment of the Readjustment Needs of Military Personnel, et al. "Access and Barriers to Care." *Returning Home from Iraq and Afghanistan: Assessment of Readjustment Needs of Veterans, Service Members, and Their Families*, National Academies Press (US), 12 Mar. 2013, www.ncbi.nlm.nih.gov/books/NBK206856. Accessed 28 Jan 2018.

DeAngelis, Tori. "More PTSD amongst Homeless Vets." *Monitor on Psychology,* American Psychological Association, Vol.44, No.3 (Mar. 2013), 22, http://www.apa.org/monitor/2013/03/ptsd-vets.aspx Accessed 18 Apr. 2018

Diagnostic and Statistical Manual of Mental Disorders: DSM-5. Arlington, VA: American Psychiatric Publishing, 2013

Fulton, Jessica J., et al. "The Prevalence of Posttraumatic Stress Disorder in Operation Enduring Freedom/Operation Iraqi Freedom (OEF/OIF) Veterans: A Meta-Analysis." *Journal of Anxiety Disorders*, vol. 31, 2015, pp98-107, doi.org/10.1016/j.janxdis.2015.02.003. Accessed 13 Feb. 2018.

Kinney, Wayne. "Comparing PTSD among Returning War Veterans." *Journal of Military Veteran's Health,* Vol. 20, No. 3 2018, pp21-23, jmvh.org/article/comparing-ptsd-among-returning-war-veterans/. Accessed 8 Feb. 2018.

McDermott, Walter F. *Understanding Combat Related Post Traumatic Stress Disorder*. McFarland & Co., 2012.

McKnight, Whitney. "New PTSD Guidelines: VA/DOD Elevate Therapy above Medication." *Clinical Psychiatry News*, Aug. 2017, p. 1+. *Health Reference Center Academic*, link.galegroup. com.ezproxy.gvsu.edu/apps/doc/A503775036/HRCA?u=lom_gvalleysu&sid=HRCA&xid=d2a2a237. Accessed 29 Jan. 2018.

Philipps, Dave. "Suicide Rate Among Veterans Has Risen Sharply Since 2001." *New York Times*, Late Edition (East Coast), 08 July 2016, A 12.ProQuest, search-proquest-com.ezproxy. gvsu.edu/docview/1802372786?pq-origsite=summon. Accessed 28 Jan. 2018.

Reisman, Miriam. "PTSD Treatment for Veterans: What's Working, What's New, and What's Next." *Pharmacy and Therapeutics*, Oct. 2016, pp 623-634, www.ncbi.nlm.nih.gov/pmc/articles/PMC5047000/. Accessed 28 Jan. 2018.

Sayer, Nina, et al. "Reintegration Problems and Treatment Interests Among Iraq and Afghanistan Combat Veterans Receiving VA Medical Care." *Psychiatric Services*, vol. 61, no. 6, Jan. 2010, pp 589-97, doi:10.1176/appi.ps.61.6.589. 29 Jan. 2018.

Slack, Donovan. "Inaccurate VA Wait Times Preclude Thousands of Vets from Getting Outside Care, Probe Finds." *USA Today*, Gannett Satellite Information Network, 3 Mar. 2017, www. usatoday.com/story/news/politics/2017/03/03/veterans-affairs-inspector-general-widespread-inaccuracies-wait-times/98693856/. Accessed 28 Jan. 2018.

United States, Department of Veteran's Affairs, "VA Suicide Prevention Program: Facts about Veteran Suicide." *US Department of Veteran's Affairs,* July 2016, www.va.gov/opa/publications/factsheets/Suicide_Prevention_FactSheet_New_VA_Stats_070616_1400.pdf. Accessed 8 Feb. 2018

"US Veterans & Military Families." *Costs of War*, Watson Institute for International and Public Affairs, Brown University, Jan. 2015, watson.brown.edu/costsofwar/costs/human/veterans. Accessed 28 Jan. 2018.

"Vietnam War Facts, Stats and Myths." *US Wings*, 2018, www. uswings.com/about-us-wings/vietnam-war-facts/. Accessed 8 Feb. 2018.

"What is EMDR?" *EMDR Institute,* 2018, www.emdr.com/what-is-emdr/. Accessed 28 Jan. 2018.

# A CASE FOR A CLEAN COOPERSTOWN

Every boy growing up in my neighborhood wore uniforms of pin-stripes, an emblazoned Old English D, or if they were truly deranged, some other team's colors. All summer long scruffy-haired bowl and buzz cuts were covered by the ball caps of our favorite clubs. And secretly, never spoken aloud with the thought that this might curse us, every boy harbored the same fantasy: that one day we would don the uniform for real and pinch hit the game seven grand slam in the ninth inning of the World Series. A benign twist on this fantasy was imagining ourselves as the players we idolized. Whether it be at a little league diamond, or a friend's backyard, we pretended to be Barry Bonds, Alex Rodriguez, or Sammy Sosa. We'd imitate them walking up to makeshift home plates before a pitch, pointing to invisible fans and guaranteeing home run balls. We made them gods. A kid doesn't know that their heroes are mortal, that they are fallible, and in a perfect world they would never have to learn this harsh truth. In a perfect world there wouldn't be congressional hearings into our favorite stars, or tell-all memoirs written exposing all the dirty secrets. In a perfect world high school athletes wouldn't feel such an overwhelming pressure to make it to the big time that they would do anything, even harm their bodies, to get there. In a perfect world, college kids wouldn't feel the need to turn to drugs to achieve their 4.0 GPAs they feel are essential to attaining the profession they desire. But we do not live in a perfect world. We live in a world where desperate people lie and cheat to gain their critical advantages, and this can be perfectly seen in the performance enhancing drug (PED) crisis that struck baseball. The steroid era, as the '90's and 2000's of the sport is now known as, is a microcosm of a societal issue that we are just beginning to realize. The frightening thing is, it is something we are starting not only to expect, but to accept. Those that once vilified and made pariahs of players that even were suspected or accused of using PEDs are softening their views. Some are even considering allowing them into the holiest of baseball shrines, The National Baseball Hall of Fame in Cooperstown, New York. If this is allowed it will not only tarnish the sanctity and pureness of a sport that has gone unchanged since its creation in the 1800's, but we are condoning as a society the mentality of "any means necessary," of winning at any cost. We will be teaching our kids that cheating is okay, and even praiseworthy, as long as you do it and you win. This cannot be allowed. We must condemn those that were found guilty of PED use, bar them from baseball's hallowed halls, and reverse a growing problem amongst our youth sports and academics. The steroid era is a black mark on baseball's rich history, and although it was a fascinating spectacle, those that participated in it should be permanently banned from entering the famed monument at Cooperstown.

There are many rationalizations made by those that think players caught using should not be punished: "everyone was doing it" or "they didn't know what they were using" or "it didn't give them that big of an edge." Perhaps the strongest argument can be made for "It's what the fans wanted to see." This is undeniably true. John-Erik Koslosky, a writer for internet investing website "The Motley Fool", argues that "steroids saved baseball." Koslosky uses league revenue to document an increased demand for "the home-run ball" during baseball's steroid era, stating "League Revenue grew from 1.4 billion in 1995 to 3.7 billion in 2001" (Koslosky). While Barry Bonds was trying to beat Hank Aaron's home run record, and Sammy Sosa and Mark McGwire were battling it out, people tuned in, in record numbers to watch offensive heroics, brought to you in part by big pharmaceutical steroids. A congressional hearing even found that the League might not have condoned its players using, but they certainly didn't mind the effects. In 2007, after an extensive congressional review of steroid use in baseball, the then Senate Majority Leader George Mitchell said in an interview with NPR: "Of course, the players who used, obviously, bear responsibility for their actions. But they did not act in a vacuum." He goes on to say further in the interview that "the owners did not press hard on the issue because they had other economic concerns" ("Mitchell"). If the players were seeing the benefits of performance enhancing drugs in their stats, the owners were seeing it in their wallets.

And the players were seeing those huge benefits in their statistics. A bleacherreport.com article shows that during the early '90's through the mid-2000's, the average number of players hitting over forty homeruns skyrocketed, as did the overall high for homeruns hit (Rymer). According to Baseballreference.com, the encyclopedia for baseball stats and knowledge, there were 17 players who hit over forty home runs, the previous high being only eight ("*For*

*Single Seasons"*). These were the League's best players, smashing records that had stood for almost a half century. And while "everyone" might not have been doing it, the pressure to compete was intense. An anonymous pitcher interviewed in GQ magazine talks about why he used: "Last season, I just couldn't throw hard anymore. All summer, I was like, 'What the hell is wrong?' I tried long-tossing, then I tried not throwing as much. I spent every day in the bullpen. It was just a disaster. Halfway through the summer, I told myself, 'If I make it to the off-season without getting released, I'm gonna friggin' do steroids, 'cause I got nothing to lose now.'" (Penn). This pitcher was not competing for the starting spot on the Yankees, but was a mere minor leaguer trying to make it into the big time. This small anecdote shows just how real the pressure to perform was. And if all it took was an injection to do it, why not? Put simply, the players saw the benefit to their careers, and the owners definitely saw it in their bottom line. No harm, no foul ball right?

Except there is a tremendous harm in consuming anabolic steroids, first and foremost to the people who use them. The National Institute on Drug Abuse lists a long catalog of physical and mental side effects. In the short term it offers mental health risks such as paranoia, extreme irritability, and delusions, while the long-term use can lead to kidney failure, liver problems, and heart illnesses to include heart attack and stroke (National Institute on Drug Abuse). Teens, the age group desperate enough to do anything to make it to the big leagues, face even greater consequences. The drug not only comes with all those same side effects, but also damages their reproductive organs and interferes with their natural growth and development (National Institute on Drug Abuse). All this leaves out the worst side effect of all: death. The number of deaths directly caused by steroids is hard to pinpoint because steroid overdose will never show up on an autopsy report. But just a quick internet search reveals the hundreds of stories of those affected. An article by T-Nation.com, a bodybuilding website and blog, lists thirty-one known steroid using bodybuilders who died before their time due to the side effects of steroids (Coluci). Then there are the more famous athletes of the WWE who have died as well: from Chris Benoit, to the Muscle Man "Oh YEAH!" Randy Savage (Harper). And finally, you have the tragic case of Taylor Hooton, a high school baseball player, who tragically took his own life. Doctors attribute his suicide to discontinuing steroids (Longman).

The people using these drugs are well aware of the risks and do it for one simple reason, the same reason the stars should not be allowed in the hall of fame: competitive advantage. They are called performance enhancing drugs for a reason after all. A *Scientific American* article examined Alex Rodriguez's steroid use and how it affected his play. "His homerun average jumped to a super-slugging 52 per season, compared with 36 during his first four seasons in the league and about 42 since. His runs-batted-in (RBI) statistics and total games played also peaked" (Hadhazy). And remember, it was during this era that stats like that, which were unheard of in previous generations of baseball, were not all that uncommon. These astounding numbers from hitters created a nuclear arms race in baseball. Not only did other hitters feel the need to compete, but the pitchers felt they had to retaliate by getting stronger and faster too. For every Barry Bonds at the plate there was a Roger Clemons on the mound. Beyondtheboxscore.com, a baseball news website, did the math on the WAR (a statistic measuring hypothetical "wins above replacement") of all pitchers across baseball and "in all of baseball history, there have been eleven qualified pitcher seasons with more than 7.5 WAR per 200 innings, and nine of them came between 1995 and 2004. Baseball's peak offensive era was also its peak pitching era" (Druschel).

The arms race that was so prevalent in the major leagues during this time, was even more rampant in the minors. Remember the anonymous minor league pitcher who admitted to steroid use? He expected nearly fifty to sixty percent of his colleagues were juicing in some way (Penn). The major leaguers were attempting to break records, their minor league counterparts were attempting to break the barrier into the big leagues. The ones who were honest and did not abuse steroids saw their peers go on to play for Yankees and Cubs while they were stuck playing for the Scranton Railriders or the Trenton Thunder. This unfair cheating by others may have robbed them of their chance at the Bigs. There is even talk of a possible collective lawsuit from minor leaguers, suing the major leagues for allowing the steroid era and costing them financially (Gillerman).

While the financial loss of the minor leaguers is tragic, the truly dark side of the steroid epidemic is the effect it had on kids. A study done by the University of Michigan revealed that during the height of the steroid era, 2003, that over 300,000 students from eighth to twelfth grade were using steroids. "The survey suggests that the rate of steroid use by high-school students increased throughout the 1990s before dropping off slightly in 2003." This is in direct correlation to the years that performance enhancing drugs rampaged through baseball ("Steroids"). The little leaguers saw their idolized heroes juicing and knew what they had to do. If they could take a little shot, they could grow up to be big and strong. And it is not just the jocks and athletes that saw the professionals using and found a way to their fame. Simple students seeking a better GPA found that they could take Adderall and they might not get bigger stronger and faster, but they would get smarter. An article written by the National Center for Research suggests that anywhere from 7 to 33% of college-aged students use study drugs (Study Drug). Baseball created a culture encouraging drug use to succeed, and the youth of our nation listened.

Clearly there was a degradation of ethics and morality among the great American pastime, which is the most damning argument against allowing known steroid users into the Hall of Fame. Rule number five on the voting ballot for Hall of Famers states "voting shall be based upon the player's record, playing ability, integrity, sportsmanship, character, and contributions to the team(s) on which the player played" ("Major League Baseball"). If we allow these players to sit alongside the likes of Hank Aaron and Babe Ruth, what are we saying of the integrity of these historical greats? Should using illegal drugs now be permissible in our criteria for sportsmanship? It is not a slippery slope if we allow these players in, it is the muddy bottom.

So, when I play at my beer league softball games now there are no longer boyish fantasies and imitations of my revered heroes, just a simple stepping up to the plate. I realize now that those major leaguers that cheated to win don't deserve our adoration, just our pity. They were caught up in a culture that they created of "all or nothing", of cheat to win. They paid the price with their bodies, as did the minor leaguers who tried to follow them, and the kids who idolized them. And while I do think that it was a cultural problem, helped along by greedy owners, the only way to end that problem is to show that it is not condoned. Let them keep their stolen records, with their asterisks of course, but we absolutely cannot allow them into Cooperstown.

*Word Count: 2161*

Works Cited

Colucci, Chris. "Big Dead Bodybuilders." *T NATION*, www.t-nation.com/pharma/big-dead-bodybuilders. Accessed 26 Mar. 2018.

Druschel, Henry. "The Improbably Transcendent Pitchers of the Steroid Era." *Beyond the Box Score*, Beyond the Box Score, 3 Feb. 2017, www.beyondtheboxscore.com/2017/2/3/14493976/clemens-maddux-martinez-johnson-steroid-era-dominance. Accessed 26 Mar. 2018.

"For Single Seasons, From 1901 to 2013, (Requiring HR≥40), Sorted by Greatest Number of Players Matching Criteria in a Single Season: Results." *Baseball-Reference.com*, www.baseball-reference.com/play-index/share.fcgi?id=VYz0G. Accessed 26 Mar. 2018.

Gillerman, Jonathan D. "Calling Their Shots: Miffed Minor Leaguers, the Steroid Scandal, and Examining the Use of Section 1 of the Sherman Act to Hold MLB Accountable." *Albany Law Review*, Winter 2010, p. 541+. *General OneFile*, http://link.galegroup.com.ezproxy.gvsu.edu/apps/doc/A226046763/ITOF?u=lom_gvalleysu&sid=ITOF&xid=d5003e01. Accessed 26 Mar. 2018.

Hadhazy, Adam. "Do Anabolic Steroids Make You a Better Athlete?" *Scientific American*, 11 Feb. 2009, www.scientificamerican.com/article/a-rod-steroids-better-athlete/. Accessed 26 Mar. 2018.

Harper, Paul. "Tragic WWE Stars Who Died Suddenly from Heart Conditions after Careers Ended." *The Sun*, The Sun, 16 Jan. 2017, www.thesun.co.uk/sport/2413111/tragic-wwe-stars-who-died-suddenly-from-heart-conditions-after-careers-in-the-ring-ended/). Accessed 26 Mar. 2018.

Koslosky, John-Erik. "How the Steroid Era Saved Baseball." *The Motley Fool*, The Motley Fool, 14 Jan. 2014, www.fool.com/investing/general/2014/01/14/we-cant-ignore-the-steroid-era-it-just-might-have.aspx. Accessed 26 Mar. 2018.

Longman, Jere. "DRUGS IN SPORTS; An Athlete's Dangerous Experiment." *The New York Times*, The New York Times, 26 Nov. 2003, www.nytimes.com/2003/11/26/sports/drugs-in-sports-an-athlete-s-dangerous-experiment.html. Accessed 26 Mar. 2018.

"Major League Baseball: Integrity, Sportsmanship and Character Create Problems for Hall of Fame Voters." *Www.ohio.com*, www.ohio.com/akron/sports/major-league-baseball-integrity-sportsmanship-and-character-create-problems-for-hall-of-fame-voters. Accessed 26 Mar. 2018.

"Mitchell: Many to Blame for Baseball's Steroids Era." *National Public Radio*, December 13, 2007, https://www.npr.org/templates/story/story.php?storyId=17222523.

National Institute on Drug Abuse. "Anabolic Steroids." *NIDA*, www.drugabuse.gov/publications/drugfacts/anabolic-steroids. Accessed 26 Mar. 2018.

Penn, Nate. "Why I Took Steroids: A Pitcher's Confession." *GQ*, GQ, 2 Sept. 2005, www.gq.com/story/baseball-steroids. Accessed 26 Mar. 2018.

Rymer, Zachary D. "Proof That the Steroid-Era Power Surge in Major League Baseball Has Been Stopped." *Bleacher Report*, Bleacher Report, 12 Apr. 2017, bleacherreport.com/articles/1648362-proof-that-the-steroid-era-power-surge-in-baseball-has-been-stopped. Accessed 26 Mar. 2018.

"Steroids and Kids; More Than 300,000 Students Between Grades 8-12 Used Steroids in 2003, Survey Found; Specialist in Youth Sports Calls Steroid Use 'A Burgeoning Epidemic'." *PR Newswire*, 12 Dec. 2004. *General OneFile*, http://link.galegroup.com.ezproxy.gvsu.edu/apps/doc/A126053298/ITOF?u=lom_gvalleysu&sid=ITOF&xid=470ed674. Accessed 26 Mar. 2018.

"'Study Drug' Abuse by College Students: What You Need to Know." *National Center for Health Research*, 1 May 2017, www.center4research.org/study-drug-abuse-college-students/. Accessed 26 Mar. 2018.

# TWO TUESDAYS IN KANDAHAR:
# MY FORTY-EIGHT HOURS IN A NEVER-ENDING WAR

The second Tuesday was October 16th. The only thing I can remember is the song that was playing before the blast: "Bodies," by Drowning Pool. It might not have been as eloquent as the songs of our Vietnam ancestors but it was ours. We didn't want a song of protest anyways; we wanted a song of provocation. It played through the headphones, its bass filled chorus screaming violence into our ears. Before we had listened to other things, Taylor Swift's "22" had been popular, and for a time Jay-Z's new album had its spot, but not now. Now we craved the anger inducing, rage filled lyrics, the screaming prayer to drop the bodies repeated over and over. I remember hearing it, reveling in it, letting its hatred fill me while driving the vehicle. I scanned the barren dessert surroundings hoping to see the enemy so I could fulfill the song's simple request, but that's all I can remember because after that my world goes black.

Underneath my vehicle the earth fissured. Maybe miles away they felt only a silent shiver, or maybe they felt nothing at all, but underneath my truck the entire world cracked, splintered, and broke apart. Black dust and smoke filled the bright blue, cloudless October sky. Where there once was a straight path of white dirt and gravel road, now there was a giant crater. Cracks in the crust of the earth resonated out from the epicenter. The ringing of the explosion sounded off the nearby mountains and echoed a haunting rendition back.

The smoke and dust settled around the truck. RPG netting fell off the sides; MREs and water bottles that had been strapped down in the back were thrown into the street. A tow-bar attached to the front of our vehicle clung on by a single welding point. Windows cracked, lights flashed, tires deflated, and the real horror began on the inside.

The blast had broken through the bottom armor sending clay earth and dust and smoke everywhere inside the cab. It was a brown and muddled haze of destruction. I lay against the windshield knocked unconscious. My gunner clung viciously to his ears trying to claw out the ringing sound. My sergeant bled from the hand and face. Nothing went unscathed. The world itself died underneath us and inside we felt its pain. A squelch from one of the other trucks came over the radio (Williams and Hoffman both claim they were the ones to say it) and said simply "Fuck Tuesdays."

By the end we had a saying, "Nothing good happens on a Tuesday." It wasn't meant to be ironic or funny – in fact it was often said with a grave seriousness. Spoken solemnly by one member of the squad others would repeat it in a sort of chant, a prayer to ward off the evil that might come out on the mission. Some of the time the prayer would work and we would return to the outpost sweaty and tired, but whole. Other times the prayer went unanswered and the mythos of Tuesdays being ominous would grow. Tuesdays were days of AK fire and grenade blasts. Tuesdays were IED explosions. Tuesdays were friends screaming in pain. Tuesdays were nightmares. Tuesdays were bad. Fucking. Days.

Maybe we left for Afghanistan on a Tuesday and that was our curse. I can't remember. I do remember the generals' speeches, before we left. All of us standing in formation listening to him calling us heroes. I remember the flags waving, the yellow ribbons pinned on to the front of everyone in the bleachers shirts, the soldiers of my company standing in formation, our fresh pressed combat uniforms not camouflaging us at all in the cheerfully warm sun. There's Sgt. Crooks, my team leader, standing next to me with his Combat Action Badge that I longed for and desired already pinned to his chest from his time in Iraq. And there's PFC Ravert, my gunner, baby faced and chubby cheeked. He would have his twenty first birthday in Afghanistan.

I was proud then, and believed everything the generals were saying. "You are our nation's heroes," "You defend the freedom of the country and of Afghanistan," . . . they might as well have said "Be all you can be," or "An army of one," their speeches were tailored straight out of the recruiting videos. I stood at the position of attention, my legs and back straight, day dreaming of the medals I would be awarded and the good I would do. I let my mind wander onto photos of handing out teddy bears to Afghan school children, of protecting them from the evil Taliban boogeymen. It felt good to be the hero, the good guy. When the speeches ended, the families gathered around to shake hands and hug, still waving those flags, still wearing those yellow ribbons, and they cried proud tears for their hometown heroes as we boarded the plane for another world.

Kandahar. Every soldier needs a war and every war needs its signature battlefield. Kandahar had the same poignant sound as Dien Bien Phu or the Chosin Reservoir. It was our Omaha, our Gallipoli, our San Juan Hill, and our Gettysburg. In a country that before 2001 only historians and Russians had paid any attention to, we would win our glory. We marched off the plane carrying weapons and equipment handed down from our Vietnam lineage. The first thing stepping out I noticed was how hot it was; I immediately started to sweat. And as I stepped into the dirt on the tarmac, a thick cloud of white dust kicked up. The uniforms that we stood so proudly in just forty-eight hours earlier were no longer clean or fresh pressed – they were dirty and sweat stained. Afghanistan had already claimed them.

A short helicopter ride from Kandahar airfield and we were placed down into our outpost in the middle of Arghandab village district. We replaced a platoon of soldiers, who hadn't had a clean uniform in over a year, as they returned home. And the circle of life, like that school bus from so long ago, went round and round. Three small tents for thirty of us, surrounded by sandbag walls and razor wire, and we called it home. A small tower made of more sandbags and plywood sat on each corner, with a heavy machine gun facing out at the village we were supposed to be there to protect. The irony was lost on the soldiers who built the outpost.

We would go out on patrols into the village, leaving from the outpost, walking or driving out its gates into the unknown, and returning without having accomplished anything but adding to miles on our boots. I did hand out a few teddy bears to kids, and enjoyed seeing them smile and run around when we gave them chocolate. At least for a little while I got to be the good guy.

The problem with heroes is that they all have their villains. Batman had Joker; Superman had Lex Luther; WWII soldiers had Nazis and G.I.'s in Vietnam had the VC. It would be so much easier if our villain was simply the Taliban, but it wasn't. It was the nation itself. It was the farmer on his small plot of land growing poppy and marijuana since before the Russians invaded that we told he couldn't. It was the religious tribal leader that we told couldn't practice honor revenge killings against his rival. The villain was us giving money to local leaders to help build a school, only to see him buy himself a new mansion. The villain was corruption, it was resistance to change. The villain was a nation that claimed a history of resisting conquering armies since Alexander the Great. And on June 19th, 2012, the first in a series of bad Tuesdays, the Villain would strike.

At four A.M. I climbed down from tower two, exhausted from eight hours of staring out at the village, watching the doorways and windows of mud brick houses remain still. My replacement, Corporal Williams, who had tiny wisps of a beard that no higher ranking sergeant bothered to correct, took over the would-be dreary task in my place. I trudged over the dirt, kicking up those signature white clouds of what we now called "moondust" as I went, to my tent. Inside I edged carefully between sleeping soldiers, trying not to wake anyone from that precious commodity of rest. I put down my weapon, took off my body armor, and laid on my cot. I set an alarm for two hours when we were set to go on a patrol in the village and immediately fell asleep. That alarm never rang.

Instead I woke up to Specialist Blake screaming. Before I could even shake off the fog of sleep there was a loud explosion and another scream to my left. Shrapnel ripped through the canvas of the tent tearing at the air inside and the early dawn sun blazed through the holes it made. That's when I heard Specialist Lee, my best friend, shout a simple proclamation: "I'm hit."

I threw my vest back on, still sticky with cold sweat from the night's guard shift, and rushed to his side. Lee was a bear of a man, and would've had a frightening appearance if it wasn't for his playful smile that was always present and a hearty laugh always echoing from him. He wasn't laughing now. He couldn't speak coherently over the din of more explosions and gunfire coming from outside, but we had been trained in first aid before we left. I quickly started a "blood sweep" my hands running along his uniform and skin, searching but hoping not to find a wet sticky spot of blood. It didn't take long to find. The first spot you search is the head and neck, and when I pressed against the sides of his throat I felt it, hot liquid pulsing through my fingers.

Gunfire ripped through the tent again, and Lee screamed once more, this time in panic instead of pain. I tried to keep him calm, joking. "It looks like you cut yourself shaving," I said, my voice wavering, the intended calming effect of the joke undercut by my nerves. I pulled the bandage out of my first aid pouch, hands shaking like I had epilepsy, and wrapped it tightly around his neck. As more grenades and gunfire forced themselves into our shelter, I crawled to Blake to do the same. He was bleeding through t-shirt that he had slept in, shrapnel from a grenade was deep in his back.

I felt helpless and ineffectual as I repeated the same action, bandaging but not healing his wound.

We were trapped inside that tent. Four more members of the squad would be hit by shrapnel or bullets and I crawled and feebly bandaged them all, while waiting for my turn to come to be wounded. The gunfire coming from right outside, the grenades pinning us down, we trained our guns on the door waiting for our tormentors to come through. Kandahar wasn't our Omaha anymore, it was our Alamo. This wasn't how it was supposed to be. In the day dreams and the general's speeches I had never been afraid. The storybook hero isn't supposed to know pain or fear.

The gunfire suddenly died down, and only the screams of the wounded remained; their cries another entity that had been absent in the reveries of my former self. We tentatively stepped out of our tents, carrying those too weak to walk. The carnage was all around us, spent shell casings, blood, and when we turned the corner from our tent to carry the injured to the trucks, we saw Tom Boyle lying dead, face down in the moondust.

Later we watched a security camera video of what had happened. Four Taliban members, dressed as Afghan Police officers we were training, were let on to the base. They had the proper credentials, badges with official numbers, and so many of these Afghan Police came and went so often that it wasn't unusual. They then proceeded to our tent area, where they threw over twenty grenades, and fired there AK 47's into us, the helpless victims inside. They managed to wound twelve soldiers, and kill Tom, before the guns in the towers that were watching the village outside so vigilantly, managed to turn inwards and kill them.

We had a funeral for Tom. There was no casket to display a torn and shredded corpse, just the simple soldier's memorial: a pair of boots, an upturned rifle, a helmet on top and dog tags hanging down. I hadn't known him at all, he joined our company right before we left, but when the twenty-one gun salute cracked in three separate volleys, I felt my world shatter and end. I didn't cry, I had shed all of my tears for Lee as he boarded a medevac helicopter. Instead of tears I stared fixedly at the ground. I felt myself grow cold in that hot Afghan sun.

After that I didn't care about being the hero, didn't want to be the good guy. The mood switched in the whole platoon. We didn't hand out teddy bears or chocolates to the kids anymore, didn't shake hands with the village elders. This is when we switched the music in our truck from Taylor Swift to Drowning Pool. We were only a month into the yearlong deployment and already the naiveté was gone. Every firefight was tinged with anger, they were opportunities for retribution. It was Us vs. Them now, and Them was anyone who wasn't Us. Afghanistan had taken one of ours, had sent twelve to the hospital, and now we were looking for any excuse to return the favor.

The Tuesdays, weeks, and months passed like that. Patrols, firefights, IEDs, but nothing matched the carnage of that first Tuesday. Like our predecessors of not just this war, but of all wars, we watched the calendars pass by slowly and dreamt of home.

And then October 16th came, and it was again Tuesday. "Bodies" playing in the headset, and me thinking: *just give me a reason.*

I woke up hours after the blast. Sgt. Crooks was lying in a cot near me and PFC Ravert was another one over, their bodies in different states of disarray. Pain radiated throughout my body, rippling from the head outwards. I tried to sit up but couldn't. A hand pressed me back and I.V. tubes held me down. The medic, an angel with golden hair, stroked my head and told me that I was okay. The thought echoed in my head. *"You're okay . . . you're okay . . . you're okay . . ."* and I remembered that people only tell you that when you're not. The world went black again.

A colonel came to my hospital bed where I was recovering two weeks later and pinned a medal on my chest, just like I had daydreamed of in that formation so long ago. He told me that this made me a hero; that I had lived the Army Values and it was all straight out of a recruiting ad. And when he stepped away I was still broken. The medal he had pinned on my chest hadn't repaired any of the damage that had been done. People filed by me, shook my hand and congratulated me on "winning" the award. Like it was a carnival prize and I had tossed the rings on to the right bottle and gotten a plush animal in return. Maybe they were right, the medal on my chest was worth about the same.

They kept me in the hospital until another unit came and replaced us, with fresh uniforms and a fresh attitude, and the circle of life continued. We boarded planes for home, carrying our dusty and dirty armor, our blood-soaked fatigues. And when we got there, the people were there waving their flags again and wearing their yellow ribbons to greet us crying tears of joy at our homecoming. They were so proud of their hometown heroes. And when they went to shake my hand and welcome me back I just wanted to turn away. I wasn't the hero they wanted, I wasn't a good guy after all.

*Word Count: 2729*

# PORTFOLIO TWO

## BY OLIVE WHITE

Initially, Olive White, an Advertising and Public Relations major from Elk Rapids, Michigan, felt overwhelmed by her first-year writing class. Like many students, she found the "most difficult part of writing these essays was starting them, since nothing is more intimidating than a blank Word document, a lack of ideas, a deadline, and a professor with high expectations." Despite her initial uncertainty, however, Olive used research, a good deal of planning, and many conversations with her instructor, Professor Tamara Lubic, to narrow down her topics. Olive says that the most important thing her writing course taught her, though, was how to revise her work. She explains, "Before taking this class, I thought a revision was fixing small grammatical errors and maybe rewording a sentence or two. After a very late night, 24 hours before the deadline, of course, I found out the hard way that significant revision is so much more than that."

Olive's first essay, "Finding Common Ground Among Uncommon People," explores the vexing issue of political polarization by responding to a recent TedTalk on the issue. Her second essay, "Gagging Ag-gag" examines the problems created by legislation that prohibits concerned citizens and whistleblowers from reporting animal mistreatment at industrialized farms. Finally, Olive reflects on a single moment in her work as a restaurant server that influenced her decision to go to college in her essay, "A Handlebar Mustache and a Crayfish Funeral." Initially, the editors of the Guide were intrigued by Olive's creative, thought-provoking titles, but as we read on, we were impressed by her deep thinking and clear writing. We think you will be, too.

### Olive's Advice for First-Year Writing Students

The best advice I can give to a WRT 150 student is to think before you write. Developing an understanding for the audience you are writing for will not only help you organize your ideas, but also allow for the reader to understand and follow your claims accurately and effectively.

# FINDING COMMON GROUND
# BETWEEN UNCOMMON PEOPLE

Society is becoming more and more politically polarized. According to a study conducted by the Pew Research Center, an unbiased American brain trust, "More people are becoming either consistently liberal or consistently conservative" (qtd. in Purcell). This study shows that individuals tend to surround themselves by those who share their same political views because it provides comfort and a sense of belonging. But because of this increased polarization between perspectives, people are not getting exposure to the opposite views. In order for an individual to be able to come to an unbiased and determined conclusion on a controversial issue, they must first have a complete understanding of every aspect of the topic, including the opposing beliefs.

While further looking into deepening one's knowledge of opposing viewpoints, I came across a TED Talk that focuses on gaining exposure to divergent views. The TED Talk, "Why it's Worth Listening to People you Disagree With," was presented by Zachary R. Wood, a Robert L. Bartley fellow at *The Wall Street Journal*. Wood states his belief that through engagement, "we may reach a better understanding, a deeper understanding, of our own beliefs and preserve the ability to solve problems, which we can't do if we don't talk to each other and make an effort to be good listeners" (Wood). Furthermore, Wood emphasizes that in order to form your own opinions, you must first understand the opinions of others. While I am in agreement with Woods' intentions of listening to what others have to say in order to come to a complete and personal interpretation of an issue, the result of his attempts to spread this view are not worth the unintended controversy.

While attending Williams College, Wood served as president of Uncomfortable Learning, a student group that sparked national controversy for inviting provocative speakers to campus. It was during his time leading this organization that Wood further developed his intense belief in the importance of, "Build[ing] empathy and understanding by engaging tactfully and thoughtfully with controversial ideas and unfamiliar perspectives" (Wood). In an attempt to make his fellow students listen to opposing viewpoints,

Uncomfortable Learning invited highly offensive political commentator John Derbyshire to speak on their own college's campus. In 2012, Derbyshire wrote an article on how to stay safe and away from blacks. In it, he offered suggestions such as: "Do not attend events likely to draw out a lot of blacks," "Stay out of heavily black neighborhoods" and "Do not act the Good Samaritan to blacks in distress." Backlash erupted almost instantaneously on social media from both staff and students alike. The resistance was so intense that the college president rescinded the invitation, much to Woods' disappointment. I most certainly agree with Wood on the fact that it is incredibly important to obtain a firm understanding of viewpoints that do not align with your own. However, I do not believe that a one-sided presentation of clearly outdated, racist, and offensive viewpoints on a college campus, or anywhere for that matter, is an effective and civil way of proving your point.

In his talk, Wood acknowledged the fierce opposition to Uncomfortable Learning. He understood that his work "hurt the feelings of many" and that for some, "listening to offensive views can be like reliving the very traumas that they've worked so hard to overcome" (Wood). Many also argue that by giving these controversial speakers a platform to spread their highly offensive ideas, it causes more harm than good. Wood addresses these counter arguments by explaining that tuning out opposing viewpoints doesn't make them go away, because millions of people agree with them. Wood also points out that "in order to understand the potential of society to progress forward, we need to understand the counterforces" (Wood). While I agree that in order to understand our own beliefs, we must first understand all surrounding viewpoints, with Woods' mindset, the weight lies more with the "giving the platform" side rather than "listening to opposing views." Uncomfortable Learning was so focused on giving the platform to insulting speakers, they overlooked the deeper problem of people's engagement with these highly offensive arguments. In any case, the majority of students who show up to presentations are most likely in favor of the speaker's argument, while the few that oppose are most likely be there to protest. The polarization between views is a major problem that cannot be solved by shoving provoking speakers in front of people's faces.

As specified by an article found on the Pew Research Center website, there has been a significant increase in partisan animosity. In each political party, "The share with a highly negative view of the opposing party has more than doubled since 1994. Most of these intense partisans believe the opposing party's policies are so misguided that they threaten the nation's well-being" ("Political Polarization"). 94% of Democrats are to the left of the median Republican while 92% of Republicans are to the right of the median Democrat (see Fig. 1). In accordance with Woods' intentions, I too believe that the only way to decrease this dramatic polarization is through agreement and understanding between the two parties.

If Uncomfortable Learning brought speakers to campus who spoke out on social problems society is faced with today that are very commonly divided across the nation, I believe that they would receive a much more positive outcome. Without the racism and public offense, groups from both sides of the argument would be more willing to converse, resulting in a much more constructive and productive product. These are the results Wood seems to be striving for.

While I agree with Wood's emphasis on learning from the other side, I would argue that discussion and debate are more effective than a unilateral lecture, especially on a college campus. A more effective approach might be to host an event where people interested can discuss and debate controversial topics. But even then, clearly outdated and racist speakers will most likely result in

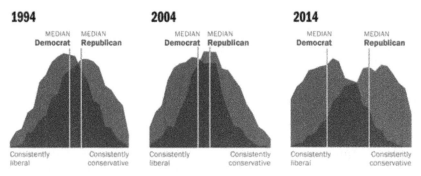

**Democrats and Republicans More Ideologically Divided than in the Past**

*Distribution of Democrats and Republicans on a 10-item scale of political values*

**1994**        **2004**        **2014**

MEDIAN   MEDIAN        MEDIAN   MEDIAN        MEDIAN        MEDIAN
**Democrat**  **Republican**   **Democrat**  **Republican**   **Democrat**     **Republican**

Consistently    Consistently     Consistently    Consistently     Consistently     Consistently
liberal         conservative     liberal         conservative     liberal          conservative

Source: 2014 Political Polarization in the American Public
Notes: Ideological consistency based on a scale of 10 political values questions (see Appendix A). The blue area in this chart represents the ideological distribution of Democrats; the red area of Republicans. The overlap of these two distributions is shaded purple. Republicans include Republican-leaning independents; Democrats include Democratic-leaning independents (see Appendix B).

**PEW RESEARCH CENTER**

Fig. 1. Democrats and Republicans More Ideologically Divided than in the Past (1994–2014) ("Growing Ideological Consistency")

more harm than good. Even though Wood addressed the resulting harm in his lecture, he failed to find commonalities between his beliefs and the opposition's. Isn't discovering a common ground and compromising with people you disagree with the key point of Woods' argument?

Wood emphasizes that in order to form your own opinions, you must first understand the opinions of others. By listening to what others have to say, one can decide for oneself what to agree and disagree with. Listening to an opposing side of an argument can leave a person feeling very uneasy and tense, especially if the subject is very intimate. According to social worker and author Eric Turner, "We like to only listen to what leaders and peers have to say in support of those areas because, otherwise, we'll be uncomfortable" (Turner). Although I am not perfect when it comes to actively seeking out opposing viewpoints, I definitely understand the benefits and can see the importance of learning the reasoning behind others' beliefs. When Wood says that "There [is] always something to learn from the perspective of others," he means that engaging with controversial ideas allows for the discovery of common ground "if not with the speakers themselves, then with the audiences they may attract or indoctrinate" (Wood). We as humans have developed a sense of security in the ideas we develop from listening to views we agree with. Wood says it best when he stated that in order "To achieve progress in the face of adversity, we need a genuine commitment to gaining a deeper understanding of humanity" (Wood). In order for society to progress forward, we need to understand the counterforces.

Wood gives a personal anecdote of a time he sat down to dinner with Charles Murray, another highly controversial and racist speaker. During their dinner, Wood explains that they had a cordial discussion on the ways in which each of them wanted to approach the issue of inequality. Their understandings on what inequality entailed were very different. But through their conversation, Woods developed a clear understanding of where Murray's conservative beliefs were rooted. Wood emphasizes that while Murray "expressed his viewpoints eloquently, [he] remained thoroughly unconvinced. But [he] did walk away with a deeper understanding" (Wood). By informing the audience of his personal encounter with opposing views, we are given a glimpse of the results Uncomfortable Learning was searching for. Without this anecdote, the audience would be left wondering what the actual effects of engagement with the other side of an argument would be.

As a whole, I agree with Wood's belief of engaging in controversial ideas. In order to come your own conclusion on a single belief, there must first be a solid understanding of every perspective of the issue. How can one come to a conclusion on their opinion if they don't understand why they believe that in the first place? Nevertheless, if Wood really wants society to start engaging in these counterforces, it should be through conversation and civil debate, not one-way presentations. Only then will humanity achieve the progress Wood intends.

*Word Count: 1521*

## Works Cited

"Growing Ideological Consistency." *Pew Research Center*, 11 June 2014, https://www.people-press.org/2014/06/12/section-1-growing-ideological-consistency/pp-2014-06-12-polarization-1-01/.

"Political Polarization in the American Public." *Pew Research Center*, 12 June 2014, https://www.people-press.org/2014/06/12/political-polarization-in-the-american-public/

Purcell, Alex. "Listening to Opposing Views." *The Shorthorn*, November 4th, 2015, http://www.theshorthorn.com/opinion/column-listen-to-opposing-views/article_761e7f48-7f65-11e5-955d-f3500efacfaf.html.

Turner, Eric. "Why it's a Good Idea to Listen to Opposing Views." *The Startup*, April 23, 2018, https://medium.com/swlh/why-its-a-good-idea-to-listen-to-opposing-views-ae2c28d68d05.

Wood, Zachary R. "Why it's Worth Listening to People You Disagree With." *TED.com*, April 2018, https://www.ted.com/talks/zachary_r_wood_why_it_s_worth_listening_to_people_we_disagree_with.

# GAGGING AG-GAG

Smiling proudly in my second-grade school photo, with my hair pulled into pigtails, I wore a red shirt, a blue headband, and a chocolate milk mustache. That picture hung in our staircase for many years, earning me the occasional taunt from a friend who would notice my dairy-made "facial hair." "A chocolate milk a day keeps the doctor away" was apparently the motto my parents lived by, for they packed me a carton in my lunch box all through elementary school. Not once did I consider where my beloved drink might be coming from. Then again, why should anyone, let alone a second grader, have to be concerned about where their food or drinks originated? It is the unfortunate truth that in the society humans are living in today, a large majority of the food people consume every day comes from factory farms. With my childhood favorite brand of milk being Fairlife, a national milk supplier, I was shocked when I came across undercover footage from the dairy farm leaked on social media in June of this year. These videos showed employees of Fair Oaks Farm, one out of the 30 livestock operations within Fairlife, punching, stomping, slamming, throwing, and breaking the bones of calves. After further investigation, I discovered an article on the Animal Legal and Historical Center website where Legislative Affairs Manager Alicia Prygoski states that this animal abuse is occurring nationwide, hidden from the public as a result of a form of legislation formally known as ag-gag laws. Prygoski explains that these laws prohibit potential whistleblowers from recording at industrialized farming operations (Prygoski). If living conditions for animals raised for slaughter need to be hidden from the public, they need to be completely reformed. Ultimately, ag-gag legislation is unconstitutional, as it violates a wide spectrum of issues Americans value such as animal welfare and First Amendment rights, as well as protects such industrial farms from public exposure and criminal prosecution while the American consumer remains unaware.

Animal welfare activists have been seeking to expose animal abuse occurring in factory farms all across the United States for years. These animal protection organizations began conducting undercover investigations in order to reveal the unsanitary conditions and animal abuse occurring in such farmsteads to the public. As stated by an article on the website of the Humane Society of the United States, an investigation of Wyoming Premium Farms, a pig plantation in Wheatland, Wyoming, resulted in the arrest of nine employees after undercover footage revealed them kicking, punching, and slamming mother pigs and their piglets ("Anti-whistleblower"). Another investigation of a cow slaughter plant, located in California, "prompted the largest meat recall in U.S. history" ("Anti-whistleblower"). Associate professor of Political Science, Pamela Fiber-Ostrow, at California State University states that "As an effective strategy that has exposed animal abuse as well as conditions threatening to public health . . . the agricultural industry has pressured legislatures to enact laws that criminalize photography at factory farms" (Fiber-Ostrow 230). Labeled ag-gag laws, Fiber-Ostrow emphasizes that "the emergence of [this] legislation targeting animal rights advocates raises important questions relevant to animal welfare . . . and freedom of speech" (Fiber-Ostrow 230). With full protection from public exposure, these factory farms are free to put profit above animal welfare.

According to an article on the *Reporters Committee for Freedom of the Press* website, the first ever ag-gag law was passed in Kansas in 1990. The article states that the law "criminaliz[ed] trespassing on a livestock facility to take pictures or video with the intent to damage enterprise" ("An Overview"). Montana and North Dakota passed their own similar laws in 1991. Montana forbid only those who had "the intent to commit criminal defamation," while North Dakota went with a more extensive constraint, prohibiting any "person without the effective consent of the owner...[to] enter an animal facility and use or attempt to use a camera, video recorder, or any other video or audio recording equipment" ("An Overview").

Because these laws have become a recent "trend," the constitutionality of ag-gag legislation has come into question. As stated in an article by The American Society for the Prevention of Cruelty to Animals, in the span of a few years, ag-gag laws have been struck down in more than 20 states for violating Americans' First Amendment rights, but as of June 2019, there are still six states that have farm whistleblowing criminalized. These states, in chronological order, are Iowa, Utah, Missouri, Idaho, Wyoming, and North Carolina ("What is Ag-gag"). As reported by Jessalee Landfried, an expert in agriculture law, whistleblowers conducting undercover investigations are protected by our country's guarantee of free speech and expression (Landfried 381). The First Amendment clearly states it "guarantees freedom of expression by prohibiting Congress from restricting the press or the rights of individuals to speak freely" ("First Amendment"). Therefore, by stifling the freedoms of the public to be knowledgeable of the origin of their food, and spread that knowledge, it is a clear violation of the Constitution.

Ag-gag legislation is protecting factory farms and their workers from criminal exposure. The ability to investigate corporate animal abuse is vitally important to not only the health of the public, but also to the safety and treatment of animals nationally. As reported by the same article found on the Humane Society of the United States website, undercover footage of Wyoming Premium Farms revealed "sick cows being dragged by chains or pushed by forklifts to be slaughtered. A significant amount of the meat from this slaughterhouse was headed to the National School Lunch Program ("Anti-whistleblower"). As a result of these videos being leaked to the public, the workers who had been conducting the abuse on the cows were fired and were reportedly charged with animal cruelty, as reported by the Humane Society of the United States (qtd. in Zelman). And in an article released by *U.S. News,* only one employee was arrested as a result of the animal brutality that took place on Fairlife farm sites ("The Latest"). In another case, an article located on the Animal Legal Defense Fund website detailed the Massachusetts farmers that were charged with more than 150 counts of animal cruelty in what has been called the largest farmed animal cruelty case (Pallotta). Animal cruelty at the property included animals housed with rotting carcasses and countless suffering from severe malnutrition. After numerous complaints from local residents, the article further explains that "many are struggling to understand how a horrific case of this magnitude could have gone on for so long" (Pallotta). These are only three farms out of the thousands located in the United States today. By silencing and penalizing whistleblowers, employees are free to torture, beat, throw, and stab animals without punishment. And as a result of ag-gag legislation, criminal behavior is being hidden from the public.

The first step in completely eradicating ag-gag laws is through public awareness. The American consumer remains uninformed on not only the actuality and seriousness of animal brutality, but most importantly, why these malpractices are being hidden from them in the first place. While the unconstitutional laws have been around since the 1990s, only recently was there  a small and short eruption in the media on ag-gag legislation. The undercover footage of Fair Oaks Farm went viral, trending on popular social media platforms such as Twitter and Instagram. And yet there was no mention of the laws that allowed for this abuse to go on for so long. As an advocate for animal rights, I had not been exposed to the truths of ag-gag laws until I deepened my research. Although these factory farms may be out of sight, they don't have to be out of mind.

While it is true that, as stated by Legislative Affairs Manager Alicia Prygoski, ag-gag laws were initially created to protect farms from trespassers looking to damage property and prevent people from entering farms for any other reason than to produce food, the damage that has occurred within these facilities, as a result of the factory practices themselves, is far worse (Prygoski). It is also argued that these videos are an unfair portrayal of the farming industry as a whole, as mentioned by Rita Lobo, macro-economic news specialist. Despite this argument, the public has a right to know about the animal abuse and violations occurring in a majority of the factories they are purchasing their food from. And while the secret reportings have had a negative effect on the image of industrialized farming, I would argue that by releasing horrific footage of the happenings inside these establishments, it encourages the enhancement of industry standards. In response to the video, an article posted on **CBS NEWS** stated that Fairlife promised to "immediately suspend deliveries and will provide more animal welfare training for employees" (O'Kane). The brand also pledged "to increase animal welfare checks and will no longer get dairy from farms that violate its animal abuse policy" (O'Kane). By eliminating ag-gag laws, agricultural institutions will be forced to regulate their management practices and conduct more thorough monitorization of their employees. And by gagging ag-gag, animal cruelty, as a result of lawmakers trying to protect factory farming industries, will be put to an end.

*Word Count: 1522*

Works Cited

"Anti-whistleblower Ag-gag Bills Hide Factory Farming Abuses From the Public." *The Humane Society of the United States,* https://www.humanesociety.org/resources/anti-whistle blower-ag-gag-bills-hide-factory-farming-abuses-public. Accessed 4 December 2019.

Fiber-Ostrow, Pamela, and Jarret S. Lovell. "Behind a Veil of Secrecy: Animal Abuse, Factory Farms, and Ag-Gag Legislation." *Contemporary Justice Review,* vol. 19, no. 2, June 2016, pp. 230-249. *Academic Search Complete,* doi: 10.1080/10282580.2016.1168257.

"First Amendment." *Legal Information Institute,* https://www.law.cornell.edu/.constitution/first_amendment. Accessed 11 November 2019.

Landfried, Jessalee. "Bound & Gagged: Potential First Amendment Challenges to Ag-Gag Laws." *Duke Environmental Law & Policy Forum,* vol. 23, no. 2, Spring 2013, p. 377–404. *HeinOnline,* https://heinonline.org/HOL/P?h=hein.journals/delp23&i=393.

Lobo, Rita. "The Pros and Cons of Ag-gags." *The New Economy,* 11 June 2013, https://www.theneweconomy.com/business/the-pros-and-cons-of-ag-gags.

O'Kane, Caitlin. "Fair Oaks Farms Under Investigation After Undercover Video Exposes Animal Abuse." *CBSNEWS,* 7 June 2019, https://www.cbsnews.com/news/after-undercover-video-exposes-animal-abuse-at-fair-oaks-farms-grocery-store-removes-products/.

Pallotta, Nicole. "Massachusetts Farmers Charged with More Than 150 Counts of Animal Cruelty." *Animal Legal Defense Fund,* 15 May 2017, https://aldf.org/article/massachusetts-farmers-charged-with-more-than-150-counts-of-animal-cruelty/.

Prygoski, Alicia. "Brief Summary of Ag-gag Laws". *Animal Legal and Historical Center,* 2015, https://www.animallaw.info/article/brief-summary-ag-gag-laws. Accessed 11 November 2019.

"The Latest: 1 Arrested on Abuse Charges at Indiana Farm." *U.S. News,* 12 June 2019, https://www.usnews.com/news/us/articles/2019-06-12/the-latest-man-sues-fairlife-brand-after-farm-abuse-videos.

"What is Ag-Gag Legislation?" *ASPC,* 2019, https://www.aspca. org/animal-protection/public-policy/what-ag-gag-legislation. Accessed 11 November 2019.

Zelman, Joanna. "Wyoming Premium Farms Employees Charged with Animal Cruelty, Humane Society Says." *HuffPost,* 6 December 2017, https://www.huffpost.com/entry/wyoming-premium-farms-charge-animal-cruelty_n_2359465.

# A HANDLEBAR MUSTACHE AND A CRAYFISH FUNERAL

Growing up, I never intended to go to college. I absolutely despised school, and the idea of going for any longer than what was required made me feel nauseous. My plan was to go to cosmetology school. It seemed easy enough and was my one-way ticket away from late nights spent writing last-minute papers on controversial TED Talks. I'm not saying I was bad at school, however. In fact, I was quite good. The topics I learned in my classes came naturally to me, so I never had to put any effort into earning a good grade. I passed my way through high school with ease, ending each year with honors. And because of my success in school, my parents pushed the idea of higher education on me, insisting it would be a "waste of talent" if I did anything else. But despite my family's expectations, I was set on a job that would require the absolute lowest amount of work. If only the past me could see where I am now.

I grew up in a small town in Michigan just north of Traverse City. With the population being just over 1,000 people, everybody knows everybody. Going to the grocery store in your pajamas was just not an option, unless you didn't care about running into old middle school crushes who avoided eye contact or past elementary school teachers who always wanted to engage in deep conversations about your life in the cereal aisle. Just down the road from the grocery store, which is just around the corner from my house, is an old Cajun restaurant called Pearl's. On the outside, Pearl's seems like nothing special. With its red paint chipping and its purple shutters barely hanging on the windows, I don't think I would stop to eat at this restaurant if I were a tourist passing through. But I am not a tourist. In fact, I am a regular, and I have been a regular at Pearl's for as long as I can remember.

My entire childhood revolved around this small restaurant. My mom was a bartender at Pearl's until I was six years old. I remember sitting at the bar one evening, my short legs dangling off the stool, barely able to touch the ground. While my mom tended to the needs of customers, I sat by myself, quietly watching her work. I remember analyzing her every gesture, movement, and facial expression. I had been focusing so hard on my mom that when my loose tooth that I had been nervously wiggling all day finally popped out and fell into my hand, I screamed in shock. I will never forget the questioning glares I received from every single person sitting in the restaurant that night. As I held out my hand, showing my concerned mom my bloody tooth, a scary, tall man with a handlebar mustache approached me. I tilted my head up to look at him, his eyes staring down at me in either anger or amusement: I couldn't tell. I thought he was going to kick me out of the restaurant or at least yell at me for being too loud, but instead he flashed a quick smile and walked away. That was the last time I ever sat at the bar.

My family and I went to Pearl's for lunch at least once a week when I was young. It became both our routine and something I looked forward to. I ordered the same thing every time, to the point where the waitresses wouldn't have to ask what I wanted. Instead, they would bring out my chicken strips almost instantaneously. One afternoon, seated next to my five-year-old brother and across from my overly tired mom in a corner booth, the same scary man approached. Towering over us, he itched his mustache with his pointer finger, then dropped a Styrofoam box on the table right in front of my brother. He winked at my mom, then walked away without saying a word. My eyes darted from the box, to my mom, to the box again, to the scary man almost around the corner, then finally back to my mom, who I noticed wore a grin from ear-to-ear.

"Open it," she said to my brother, who almost immediately lunged his grubby hands at the box and lifted the lid. He gasped with excitement, his eyes lighting up the same way they did on Christmas morning. I leaned over to get a look inside the box, but what I saw made me shriek with disgust. Crawling around inside that white container was a live crayfish. Its eyes were beady and black, and its shell was bright red. Its pinchers were bigger than its head, and because of that, I wanted absolutely nothing to do with it.

"I think I'll call him . . . Snuggles," he said, his face three inches away from the crayfish. We took Snuggles home with us, but he only lived about a day. A funeral was held for him in our backyard and I'm sure the whole two people that attended would say it was a beautiful service.

As I grew older, my once weekly dinners at Pearl's turned monthly, to a few times a summer, to once a year if I was lucky. My mom got a new job and my brother no longer had any interest in crayfish. At the end of my junior year of high school and as a result of my shopping addiction, I was in dire need of money, and, therefore, a job. Without talking to me first, my mom set up an interview at, guess where? That's right, Pearl's New Orleans Kitchen. I was furious. I wanted a job that would be easy and wouldn't require any hard work. Pearl's was not that job. When the day came for my interview, I was a nervous wreck. When I walked in the restaurant, I scanned the room. The chairs were still on the tables and only one of the lights was turned on. As I continued to scan, my eyes stopped upon a cup of coffee sitting on a table, the steam rising above the top of the booth. I figured that is where my interview was going to be, so I went and sat down. All of a sudden, from around the corner, came that scary, tall, man with the handlebar mustache. My heart dropped and the butterflies in my stomach multiplied. He sat down in front of me without saying a word. I can't remember how I answered his questions, but at the end of the interview, he told me I got the job. And that was when he introduced himself as my manager.

By the end of the summer, I was working full time at Pearl's. It was exhausting, to say the least, and I hated every second of it. I couldn't understand how my mom worked there for so long. The customers were rude, the servers were even worse, and hosting while on a two-hour wait was beyond stressful. I forgot to mention that Pearl's is busy every single day. Customers will wait for hours just to get a table. I was constantly surrounded by dramatic waitresses that would rant about their personal life and complain about their lack of money. I remember one night, a particularly rude waitress decided to unload her apparently very bottled-up feelings on me. Her soliloquy began on the topic of her and her husband's divorce, then quickly shifted to the mountain of bills she had to pay when she got home later that night. The grand finale of her rant, however, centered around her hatred for Pearl's.

"I think if I spend one more minute in this hell-hole I will jump off a bridge," she whined as she placed her head in her hands. I stood very still, trying not to look as uncomfortable as I felt.

"I . . . um . . . don't actually . . . um . . . think you should do that," I said after at least 30 seconds of awkward silence. And with that, she walked away as quickly as she came. It was situations like these that became common interactions while working at Pearl's. Their stress stressed me out, but because I spent almost all summer with them, their problems turned into norms. It seemed like it was normal to have a life where one is constantly worried about money, so that became my expectation for my own future, until one evening when everything changed.

It was around 8:00 pm, when Pearl's starts slowing down for the night. I was running the wait list while the other hostesses sat people at tables. Customer after customer came in, most grumpy per usual. Servers had been yelling at me because they weren't getting enough people in their sections all night, and all I wanted to do was go home. Standing at the hostess stand, waiting for more people to come in, I reorganized the already organized menus to make myself look like I was working hard. I heard the door open and I looked up. A couple had just walked in the restaurant. Holding hands, they approached my stand. They were young, no older than 25. They were both dressed very fancy, very unlike the attire most customers show up in. The woman wore a tan button-up coat and black heels while the man dressed in a white dress shirt with a black tie. While they ate dinner, I observed them as they joked with each other. Their energy was so much different than any other customer I had talked to. They seemed so carefree and secure with their lives. They seemed calm and put together, so unlike all the adults I was surrounded by every day. As I watched, the young woman reached into her Louie Vuitton purse and pulled out a sparkly pink tube of lip gloss. As she placed the tube back in her bag, I noticed a shiny metal keychain hanging on the zipper. Reflecting the overhead light, I could make out the letters "UofM." She must have noticed my curious gaze, for she turned to look at me. Startled, I looked away quickly, pretending to be deep in thought while scanning the room. As they made their way out the door after finishing their meal, the woman turned to look at me.

"Have a great night," she said, before following her husband outside. I was too nervous to respond. But as I watched the couple grab hands in the parking lot through the glass door, I felt a sense of determination come over me. Not only did I feel determination for my future, but also to live a life without the hardships of money, just like that young couple. I wanted their life. I knew then that I did not want to live like my mom or the grumpy middle-aged women who complained about their money problems and family issues all day. And I knew how I would achieve this life.

The idea of college is intimidating. I never in a million years thought I would be sitting in my college dorm room, on my college campus, writing a paper for my college class. If I hadn't have been working that night, or that young couple had gone to get pizza for dinner, I would not be getting a higher education. Although my interaction with this young wealthy couple seems small and random, that night I realized that I would never achieve the future I wanted for myself by taking the easy way out. I took control of my life and applied for colleges at the beginning of my senior year. I am not saying I enjoy school any more than I did when I was younger, but I have come to appreciate that with hard work comes success, and every paper or exam that makes me want to drop out of college brings me one step closer to the successful life I am striving for.

*Word Count: 1993*

# PORTFOLIO THREE

## BY AVERY WISSMUELLER

Avery Wissmueller, a native of West Bloomfield, Michigan, used her first-year writing class as an opportunity to write about the issues she cares about the most. Avery's first essay is an oral history, titled "Retracing History," which narrates one man's search to learn about his uncle, a US Air Force pilot who died in WWII. For her second and third essays, Avery used her passion for the environment—she's a Natural Resource Management major with minors in Biology and Environmental Studies—to explore the impact humans have on the natural world. In "Dying to be Green," Avery studies the practice of environmentally conscious and sustainable burials. Her third essay, "Agriculture: Made with Artificial Ingredients," identifies problems with the practice of monocropping (growing the same crop on the same piece of land every year), and offers more sustainable solutions, such as Grand Valley's Sustainable Agriculture Project.

As a student in Professor Dauvan Mulally's class, Avery found that her writing skills improved significantly through the consistent revision of her papers. She said this revision practice helped her "refine [her] writing habits" so that she had a more productive and effective writing process. Her favorite part of this class was the research, and she has found many benefits from the research experience she gained. In Avery's words: "The research skills I gained has significantly benefited my abilities in writing heavily research-based papers that are required in a majority of my classes."

# RETRACING HISTORY

*As told by Matthew Tijan*

As I strapped myself into the well-worn leather seat of the World War II bomber plane, I stared out the window, envisioning an engine erupting with a thick cloud of black smoke, bullet holes still red hot from 50-caliber shells. As my knees and chest strained to pull me closer to the window, I remembered the pilot's rule: "stay seated until the plane has reached cruising altitude." As I continued to gaze at the propeller's steady pace, the deep melodic hum from the engines brought me back to thinking about Ed again. I realized that to my uncle, the inflamed and failing engine was no daydream. My mind began to race with questions: *how did he learn the operations of everything? What were his feelings when he climbed into the gunner's seat? Where would he have jumped?* A cool shiver washed over me, I was left in a state of perplexity.

My uncle enlisted in the Air Force in October of 1943 when he was 18 and served for about a month before he passed away. The only details I knew about him were where he was stationed, his task of operating the ball turret, and the general story of how his parachute failed as his plane crashed. When I asked my parents about who Ed was they would only give me curt and ambiguous responses. The smiles on their faces would fade to a pair of cold and expressionless masks. Clearly, my uncle's past hit home in the heart of my father, but my siblings and I could never understand why it was something we simply could not ask about. Today, I can only speculate that my dad's repressed memory of Edward clouded his ability to relive the good ones. It was not until three years ago that my thirst for knowledge about Edward was finally satisfied. My father stopped by my home to visit my wife Monica and I and to catch up with his grandkids. As we stepped outside, he approached each of my family and I with a single outstretched arm to greet us with a hug, but concealed underneath his other arm was a dusty, misshapen cardboard shoe box with "Edward" scribbled on the lid. After my family retreated back inside, my dad leaned in closer and in a soft and genuine tone, he said, "I wanted you to have this."

"What is it?" I ask as I try to gather what could possibly be inside.

"It's all of your uncle's belongings, I know it isn't much but the men at the bunkers tossed most of his stuff right after Ed died." As he said this, I scanned his face for any sign of grief or discomfort but found nothing.

"Oh, thank you, but why did they do that?"

"They did it to everyone who died. While the flight men were out they would go find the personal belongings of whoever died and get rid of them. It saved his friends from having to grieve over his belongings" he said as he placed the dilapidated box into my hands.

I was taken aback by this information, what a sad thing to go through: losing a good friend and then coming back wanting to find something of his to remember him by, but only to find it empty. It was almost as if he had never existed. Eventually, we went inside and sat down at the dining room table. Although I acknowledged my father's dialogue with the occasional "mhm" or by nodding my head, my eyes kept drifting towards that box. "Go ahead and open it already. I can tell it's killin' ya," my dad laughed. I must have made my excitement more obvious than I had thought. As I pried open the lid of the box, I unveiled a pile of yellowish and faded personal family letters from 1945. I carefully picked them up, fearful that the 70 year old paper would disintegrate in my hands. My eyes began to follow the lines of cursive ink. His words were warm and reassuring, unlike what was going on around him at the time. Under the letters was a brass medallion encased in a translucent plastic box. I rubbed my thumb over its teardrop shape. The medallion had a royal purple background and in the foreground was the silhouette of what looked like an army general. Lastly, an Air Force ring was upside down, shoved deep into the corner of the box. The thick silver ring had been engraved with wings on the raised center with barely legible words. Out of habit, I slipped it on and it fit me perfectly. At this moment, my interest in rediscovering who my uncle was reached its peak. I needed to know more. That night, with a simple Google search, I stumbled upon a crash report from February of 1945 of Ed's bomber plane, "Big Poison." The page was flooded with information regarding all the men involved in the crash and where the crash site was located, which eventually led me to a link describing how a 55,000-pound bomber plane, after being shot down by enemy fighter planes, destroyed parts of a small farm town, injuring several people and killing a little boy as it crashed into rural England. Despite my shocking discovery, the article still did not help me discover who Ed was. I needed to take this into my own hands. I wanted to know what it was like to walk a mile in his shoes, knowing that no one in my family had been over to London gave me all the more reason to fly there. After so many years of trying to learn about the mysterious past of my Uncle Edward, I finally had the chance to become closer to my uncle and the war that has so far been kept out of my father's stories.

After two years of festering curiosity, my wife and I finally reached the quaint town of Eye, England where my uncle was stationed in December of 1944. I felt a pounding in my chest as I dried my clammy hands on my jeans. I took a deep breath to calm myself down as we traversed down the sidewalk to find our rental car. Although the town was small, people hustled and bustled among the cobblestone streets. We passed along 18th century styled buildings built with fiery red bricks, catching a whiff of freshly baked bread, until we met up with a man named Fred, our tour guide for the day. Propped up against what looked like a WWII era Jeep was a stocky gentleman in a dark leather jacket. While his back was to us, I was able to make out the white stitching that contrasted sharply from his chocolate bomber jacket. "Big Poison" was stitched on the upper back and below it was my uncle's plane releasing bombs over a Nazi swastika. My breath was cut short; *that was his plane. What are the odds out of all the regiment bomber planes*? The thudding in my chest returned. I scrambled for the right words to tell Fred about the coincidence. We parked the car and made our way across the empty street towards him. He gestured for us to enter the pub we were standing in front of. A sign with "The Swan" in dark green lettering hung from the brick building. As Fred held the door for us, we stepped over the old and creaky wooden floor until we reached the center of a dimly lit room. It was musty, and the white walls were paneled from floor to ceiling with dark wood. The pub was a single room with a couple of tables with mismatched wooden chairs, a giant brick fireplace, and only three chairs at the bar.

As I pulled out a chair facing the wall, I noticed a picture frame of an airplane crash from World War II that happened right outside the pub. It was strange to be ordering drinks in a former war zone. At first, Fred kept the conversation to bland small talk, but as soon as we got our beers he unleashed a barrage of World War II stories on us as if he was dying to get them off his chest. As he continued to discuss his interest in the American involvement during the war,

I was itching to tell him that my uncle flew on Big Poison. I worried that maybe there were other "Big Poison" bomber planes and that Fred's jacket was just a coincidence. Playing it safe, I decided to ask him where he got his leather jacket. With a knowing smile, Fred replied "Oh yeah, I remember you from all those emails about Big Poison. I saw a photo of one of those pilots wearing one and thought it was so awesome that I had one custom made for myself." As we finished up and paid our bill he told me, "Hey, when we get outside why don't you try it on for size?" I could not shake my head yes fast enough. Back outside I listened to Fred talk about Chrysler's role in providing Jeeps for the war effort. My hand drifted over the vehicle's hood, passing over the white star. As Fred began to wiggle out of the jacket my excitement began to mount. I slipped my arms through the smooth leather and adjusted it around my shoulders. Even though I knew that the jacket was not one of my uncle's lost artifacts, I felt strange with it on; like a son in his father's suit coat, as if I was not worthy of it of what it stood for.

We stepped into the doorless Jeep and began our mission. As we rode through Eye, Fred pointed out every building we saw and gave its historical importance. He pulled out an old photo of the town from the 1940s and it was identical to what it looked like today, 75 years later. We first made our way towards the Royal Air Force base where Edward was stationed. The gloomy weather added to the eeriness of the abandoned landscape. The runways crisscrossed an otherwise barren field and the barracks were no longer there. When we came to a stop, Monica and I stepped out onto the paved runways. I could not believe that I was there. The fact that I was standing where my late uncle spent his time protecting our country seemed surreal. As we neared the end of the runway we passed a dilapidated white building with cobalt blue doors and shutters. Fred explained that was where the parachutes were assembled during the war. My heart sank. Ed's parachute failed when he tried to use it to save himself, but if it were assembled correctly, maybe he would have survived and would have been able to tell me his story himself. We continued our voyage to the memorial center dedicated to the 490th bombardment group my uncle served in that was stationed in Eye. In a cleared grass patch, no wider than 15 feet across were two adjacent wooden memorial benches. At the far end of the lot was a dark marble headstone inscribed with the 250 names of the 490th bombardment group. Words of remembrance of how important this group was for serving was etched into the thick marble. I read the words slowly and thoroughly. To the right of the headstone were all the names of the men that were a part of this heroic group. My eyes scanned for the last names starting with the letter T, while my finger skimmed down the laundry list of names until it landed on my uncle's name: *Sargent Edward Tijan.* I still could not believe he was a part of this at 19 years old. I took in a deep breath and nodded my head down in remembrance of the fallen heroes.

I turned back around to Fred quietly informing Monica how the memorial came together. Fred gave me a nod and motioned for us to get back into the Jeep. This was the part of the trip for which I had the most anticipation. As the old brakes of the Jeep squeaked to a halt, I gazed in wonder at the enormous entrance to the lair of the beast. We had reached the hanger. As I stepped into the building, I was shaken by the sheer magnitude of the gun-toting behemoth that stood before me. The fuselage, wings, and nearly the entirety of the plane's body were a silvery chrome, an appearance only further emboldened by its bright red tail and USAF insignia on the doors. Even as I strolled under the pair of massive engines, I was skeptical of whether such an ancient instrument of war could still clear the runway. As I came closer to the stainless-steel giant, I could see into the cockpit, a clear dome guarded by a vicious looking turret. I took a deep breath and made my way towards the stairs that led us into the plane. As Fred lead me past a flank turret loaded with belts of high caliber machine gun rounds, I marveled at what kind of danger that Ed must have flown against to require a bomber with so much fortification. As more passengers filed into the cabin, the pilot instructed us to sit down on the seats that lined the body of the plane. My eyes began wandering along the dim interior, it was lined with thick cables, heavy machinery, and parts with functions that I could not even identify. In the middle of the aisle way was a round piece of metal with a glass shield sticking out of the floor. Connected to it were two metallic arms used for feeding the ammunition belts that disappeared into the hole. *That's the ball turret.* I was itching to get out of my seat and check it out.

I sat at the edge of my seat anxiously waiting until we reached cruising altitude. Finally, when we were given the go-ahead, I got up to inspect the ball turret. A crowd of people had circled around it, blocking my view. Although I desperately wanted to see the type of weaponry that my uncle had manned in World War II, I decided to bypass the crowd in the center of the plane and pushed my way to the cockpit. At the front of the plane, I squeezed into a small opening where I could see the full expanse of buttons, dials, and altitude gauges, none of which I could understand. Just under the cockpit, I had a chance to look out what appeared to be a viewing dome. I could see below as we passed over miles of farmland, as well as to the side and above me. The only thing obstructing my vision was the massive gun station in the center of the glass. I felt like I was about to fall out of the plane. One of the tour guides must have noticed my interest because he approached me and said, "You know you can have a seat in there if you'd like." As I sat down the tall lanky gentleman asked if I had any questions and I told him that I did. I mentioned that during my uncle's service in the 490th bombardment group, his pilot had tried to "feather the engine" as the plane went down. The gentleman began to explain that feathering meant when an engine failed the pilots would try to turn the propellers a certain way so that the wind would catch and spin them like a pinwheel which could help restart the engine. I was blown away by how much I had learned in the past day. When I returned to the middle of the plane, I was relieved to see that the crowd around the ball turret was gone. I bent down and tilted my head slowly back and forth to try and to get a better view. It was such a small compact space, I could not imagine how hot it must have been in there while wearing a heavy bomber uniform. I assumed Ed was a smaller guy because someone who was over 5'10 probably would not have fit. There was a small window in front of the chair for him to look out and shoot enemies. Seeing this in person blew me away, learning so much information about Uncle Ed made him seem more like a real person than just a faded memory. I forced myself to look away, pushing the lump in my throat and the tears in my eyes down just as my dad had done with the memory of his brother. While most who flew on the plane gazed in awe at the guns and the massive engines, I looked through the ball turret and saw Ed for the first time.

*Word Count: 2823*

Work Cited

Tijan, Matthew. Telephone interview. 4 Sept. 2018.

# DYING TO BE GREEN

In March of 2016 at TEDxOrcasIsland in Washington State, Katrina Spade, founder of Recompose, a corporation devoted to the alternative option of human burial through composting, shares her idea of utilizing natural decomposition processes for human disposal. In her TEDxTalk, "When I Die, Recompose Me," she discusses the modern burial and embalming process and how its substantial environmental footprint can be reduced by instituting human composting as a sustainable alternative.

Spade begins her presentation by sharing an anecdote of when she was in college studying architecture. During her experience at Haverford College, she began to ponder the idea of what would happen to her body after she died. While Spade references the dreary implications that the thought of death may bring, she emphasizes the role that traditional methods have in perpetuating the idea that funerals are associated with a time of mourning. Almost fifty percent of Americans opt for conventional burial, a process that includes embalming the body with formaldehyde and methanol in order to kill decomposing bacteria. Additionally, Spade points out how many natural resources are consumed by traditional burial stating that "in US cemeteries, we bury enough metal to build a Golden Gate Bridge, enough wood to build 1,800 single family homes, and enough formaldehyde-laden embalming fluid to fill eight Olympic sized pools." In addition to the concern of contamination and the expenditures of resources that could be used in more economically beneficial areas, Spade expresses concern for the rise of cremation rates. As space in cemeteries dwindles, more individuals are choosing cremation as their preferred method for disposing of a body. She further explains that many people erroneously opt for cremation in pursuit of a more ecological method of body disposition. Spade makes the case that cremation is both a source of pollution and a hindrance to the natural process of decomposition by offering statistical evidence: "Cremations in the United States emit a staggering 600 million pounds of carbon dioxide into the atmosphere annually." With the degradation of the ozone and the quality of breathable air at stake, Spade's TED Talk illuminates the effect that the current American burial system has on the environment, giving relevance to her new proposal of institutionalized human composting.

In addition to expressing a practical concern for human and environmental health, Spade hopes to benefit the Earth without harshly challenging the traditional norms that are ingrained in American society. Using the commercially practical and environmentally sustainable process of livestock decomposition as inspiration, Spade began her design for human composting facilities. The buildings will contain spaces for memorial services to provide comfort to families while the bodies of loved ones are prepared. Additionally, there will be a large central column filled with wood chips to house the cotton shrouded bodies for decomposition. Through an aerobic process, bacteria break down the nitrogenous body within 30 days, producing a nutrient-rich soil. Overall, Spade is optimistic about reinventing traditional funerary practices and plans to create a practice that is meaningful, as well as practical in an increasingly endangered global environment. As traditional burial and cremation processes become less sustainable, a shift to institutionalized human composting grows ever more necessary as a means of conserving resources.

Spade's advocacy for a more sustainable and environmentally conscious approach to human burial practices is an important idea due to increasingly limited space in cemeteries, the depletion of resources, and use of toxic chemicals. I agree with Spade's philosophy that funerary practices should allow a person to benefit the Earth rather than contribute to its degradation. With an exponentially rising human population, the Earth's finite resources are steadily depleting. The use of decomposition eliminates the need to dig a hole six feet underground, line it with cement, and bury a body in an expensive casket for eternity. Additionally, Spade's talk reported that possible contamination can result from burial as chemicals from the embalmed body leach into the soil and aquifers, polluting the public water supply. In addition to water contamination, the air we breathe is at risk. According to the International Agency for Research on Cancer, "formaldehyde is carcinogenic to humans and individuals who have potential for occupational exposure to formaldehyde in [the] air are subjected to high concentrations of this chemical, which can cause various health problems" (qtd. in Cruz 24123). This research supports that Spade is not only correct about how damaging that formaldehyde is to the environment, but also to human health.

While the processes associated with traditional burial are toxic and wasteful, most modern funerals also carry a heavy price tag. As cemeteries and the resources they require have become limited, the prices for burial have risen. For example, at Lynch & Sons Funeral Directory of Walled Lake, Michigan, the average funeral cost is $5,800, which includes the funeral and memorial services, embalming, and the transfer of a body to the designated cemetery (Whalen). However, the extra expense of burials is only a small part of the large overall cost associated with the modern funeral. A study included in *Kiplinger's Retirement Report* explains that funeral expenses in the United States costs an average of $7,000 per deceased (Kane 16-17). Spade projects that: "each human composting would cost about $2,500, a fraction of the price of conventional burial" due to the comparatively lower expenses of the labor and materials required to conduct a memorial (qtd. in Einhorn). These figures bolster Spade's argument, showing that a natural death process that renders the use of a headstone, elaborate casket, or exorbitant amounts of embalming fluid unnecessary.

In addition to cutting the amount of resources expended during traditional burial, composting also challenges the ecological efficiency of cremation. While some suggest that cremation is a "greener" and cheaper alternative, the reality is that the heating process and its byproducts are unsustainable. The process of cremation uses energy-intensive heat to disintegrate the hair and flesh, leaving the inorganic remains of bones as ash (Chamberlain et al.). In order to produce energy, cremation facilities draw heavily from the Earth's finite fossil fuels. In Spade's presentation she mentions that American crematoriums produce 600 million pounds of carbon dioxide, not only exhausting the Earth's resources but also contributing to the accumulation of greenhouse gases in the atmosphere, encouraging climate change. In addition to harming the planet, cremation poses a threat to human health. When a body is burned, the mercury from the fillings vaporizes. After mercury is released into the atmosphere it can return to the Earth through acid rain where it can percolate into aquifers and other bodies of water (Correll). This can result in the bioaccumulation of mercury which can occur in fish, making them toxic for human consumption. When mercury enters the human body, it damages the nervous system and poses a threat to child development (Correll). This information allows for a new perspective to be considered when advocating for cremation.

As more Americans reach this same realization, a green revolution has been sparked to reinvent traditional funerary practices. As Katrina Spade leads this movement, her idea to commercially compost human bodies is making headlines. Her idea eliminates the need for toxic fluids, burying perfectly good resources, and using high energy heat. All that is required are wood chips, oxygen, and bacteria. In the article "Returning the Dead to Nature" Catrin Einhorn, a journalist for *The New York Times*, discusses Katrina Spade's Urban Death Project. In the article, Spade states that after several weeks the body will break down into compost that would fill a three by three-foot box. She suggests this compost could be given to families and they could use it as they see fit, such as utilizing it as nutrient dense soil for a newly planted tree. While Spade's ideal picture of a greener funeral industry may seem as though it is without flaws, there are many cultural barriers that should be taken into consideration when attempting to make such a drastic change to funeral practices.

Despite Spade's lack of attention to the pre-established traditions that are ingrained in public opinion, they are the primary reason that her plan has not yet taken off. Although data shows that "In 2015, 64 percent of adults above 40 [years old] said they would be interested in green funeral options..." the funeral industry maintains a tight grip on American consumers. Additionally, 87 percent of adults over the age of 40 who had previously been involved in selecting a funeral provider would choose the same one for a future need, and 92 percent would make similar arrangements in the future ("FAMIC Study"). This response is likely a result of the ideology marketed to consumers by the funeral industry: that continuing to bury and cremate bodies is the most respectful way of honoring a past loved one. The funeral business poses large obstacles for the further development of alternative burial choices such as Spade's idea for human composting. Since such a large percentage of people continue to practice traditional burial, funeral industries have little incentive to uproot their firmly established facilities in pursuit of a developing, yet comparatively small demographic of compost supporters. Although the idea of composting human bodies may seem like an unfamiliar idea, traditional burial practices first emerged during the Civil War, due to the introduction of technological innovations and rise in economic affluence (Beard and Burger 47). Therefore, natural methods of disposition is a return to a fundamental technique that humans have been practicing for millennia. When faced with the idea of human compost, many members of the public form negative stigmas against processes that violate the norms they have been brought up around. These negative stigmas, such as the one that a commenter states on Spade's Urban Death website: "A pile of bodies is usually called a 'mass grave.' Please stop what you're doing" (Einhorn), can exemplify how established traditions are difficult to break. While the idea of human composting can sound morbid, it is the most organic way of going about the disposal of a corpse. These barriers pose as opportunities for greater awareness and positive change towards a greener perspective of death.

Although the traditional funerary practices that most Americans revert to have been deeply institutionalized in the United States, Spade's ideal image of "death care" strives for a more environmentally sustainable approach. Using nature as her guideline, Spade aims to reduce both the cost to the consumer and the strain on resources regarding the American funeral. While the process of human composting may have a short-term effect on funeral directories that utilize the embalming process, it will undoubtedly produce long-term benefits to future generations through a healthier environment, reduced strain on natural resources, and increasing economic benefits.

*Word Count: 1770*

## Works Cited

Beard, Virginia R., and William C. Burger. "Change and Innovation in the Funeral Industry." *OMEGA–Journal of Death and Dying*, vol. 75, no. 1, 2015, pp. 47., doi:10.1177/0030222815612605.

Chamberlain, Clive, et al. "Cremation Process." *Encyclopedia of Cremation*, edited by Douglas J. Davies, and Lewis H. Mates, Ashgate Publishing, 1st edition, 2005. Credo Reference, https://ezproxy.gvsu.edu/login?url=https://search.credoreference.com/content/entry/ashgtcremation/cremation_process/0?institutionId=222.

Correll, DeeDee. "Cremation Harms the Environment." *Disposal of the Dead*, edited by Diane Andrews Henningfeld, Greenhaven Press, 2009.

Cruz, Nicholas Joseph Tavares Da, et al. "Environmental Impacts Caused by Cemeteries and Crematoria, New Funeral Technologies, and Preferences of the Northeastern and Southern Brazilian Population as for the Funeral Process." *Environmental Science and Pollution Research*, vol. 24, no. 31, Nov. 2017, pp. 24123., doi:10.1007/s11356-017-0005-3.

Einhorn, Catrin. "Returning the Dead to Nature." *New York Times*, 14 Apr. 2015, p. D1(L). *Opposing Viewpoints in Context*, http://link.galegroup.com/apps/doc/A409516167/gvalleysu&sid=OVIC&xid=86fd00fb.

"FAMIC Study." Funeral and Memorial Information Council, www.famic.org/famic-study/.

Kane, Mary. "Smart Moves When Facing Funeral Costs." *Kiplinger's Retirement Report*, vol. 25, no. 6, June 2018, pp. 16–17. ezproxy.gvsu.edu/login?url=http://search.ebscohost.com/login.aspx?direct=true&db=bt&AN=129660314&site=ehost-live&scope=site.

Spade, Katrina. "When I Die, Recompose Me." *TED.com*, Mar. 2016, http://www.ted.com/talks/katrina_spade_when_i_die_recompose_me.

Whalen, Mary. Telephone interview. 23 Nov. 2018.

# AGRICULTURE: MADE WITH ARTIFICIAL INGREDIENTS

Many Americans are familiar with the image of a happy family cruising through the rural countryside, children gazing out the window as the rays of the rising sun weave through seemingly endless rows of corn. However, after taking a deeper look into the consequences of monoculture, the ever-expansive fields of crops that dot the American landscape begin to lose their charm. Although modern agricultural practices have become more efficient, maximizing yields in order to feed the ever-growing world population, a barrage of long-term effects threatens the sustainability of a healthy environment for future generations. More specifically, the technique of monocropping: the continual practice of growing a single crop on the same land year after year, poses the significant threat of soil depletion. Additionally, large-scale production of a specialized crop increases reliance on pesticides and fertilizers while decreasing genetic diversity in crops. Conversely, Grand Valley State University's (GVSU) Sustainable Agriculture Project (SAP) challenges monoculture practices with sustainable techniques that promote ecological responsibility. However, many small farms continue to join their larger counterparts by turning to monoculture in pursuit of the cheapest and easiest methods of farming. In order to lessen the environmental impact of monoculture, the farming industry must utilize more natural methods of farming and take steps to avoid the economic allure of specializing in only one type of crop.

Since monoculture is noticeably damaging to the environment, the fact that it is practiced by so many small and large-scale agricultural operations may initially seem puzzling. However, the immediate benefits of crop specialization have attracted large industries and have subsequently forced small farmers to adapt. The history of monoculture in America can be dated back as early as the Colonial Period, during the heavy production of tobacco. However, these practices became more popular in the 20th century with the development of advanced agricultural technologies (Ivey 930). When farmers grow only one type of crop, such as corn, soybeans, wheat, cotton, and other grains, it allows them to specialize in the techniques and machinery needed for the crop, cutting the expenses required for a broader range of equipment. This creates greater efficiency and allows for larger crop yields which maximize profits, making monoculture an easy economic choice for struggling small-scale farmers. Additionally, the United States government offers financial grants through subsidy programs such as the Price Loss Coverage (PLC) program and the Agriculture Risk Coverage (ARC) program (Alizamir et al.). These programs help keep market prices low and protect the farmer's income, further incentivizing the practices of industrial agriculture. However, these programs contribute to the overproduction of crops which exhausts the nutrients in the soil, ultimately harming the environment.

While many members of the monoculture industry may be aware of the harmful environmental effects of such a practice, these consequences may not offer enough motivation for a farmer to switch to sustainable methods due to the immediate risks associated with changing techniques. As expressed by Kelly Parker, a director of the Environmental Studies Program at Grand Valley State University, switching from traditional practices to more ecologically responsible methods involves a ". . . significant investment of time, education, and re-tooling, and if farmers don't get it right, the cost of a year or two of failure could bankrupt a farmer" (Parker). While sacrificing financial gain for greener methods of agriculture may not initially benefit an individual's enterprise, the farming industry as a whole will eventually suffer long-term environmental turmoil.

As farmers try to preserve their short-term financial interests, widespread monoculture encourages the introduction of chemicals to the local ecosystem and will lead to long term environmental consequences. Monoculture is highly dependent on the utilization of pesticides, a group of chemicals that are used to kill living things that eat or destroy food crop (Harrison et al. 115). A field of genetic uniformity, such as a monocrop field, poses a large and relatively easy target for pests and disease due to the high nutrient content available which allows them to thrive. To prevent widespread disease and destruction of the entire crop field, pesticides are coated over the fields year-round. So much so that over time, the pests have developed genetic resistance to many of the pesticides, resulting in the production of new, more potent strains of pesticides and increased application in order to eliminate damage. Farmers who use pesticides can become locked into the unsustainable practices of agriculture due to the heavy costs of new chemicals. This continuous cycle of blanketing pesticides on fields wreaks havoc on the surrounding soil's nutrient composition. As chemicals build up in the soil, they kill microbes, the organisms that break down organic materials and absorb nutrients, ultimately depleting the soil. When soil becomes riddled with chemical pesticides, the plants that previously held it in place die off, allowing loose particles to be blown away by the wind or carried downstream from runoff where it contaminates surrounding water sources.

This chain of events can also adversely affect human health, which is further explained by agricultural economic researchers: Clevo Wilson and Clem Tisdell, "According to the Food and Drug Administration approximately 35% of the foods purchased by consumers have detectable levels of pesticide residues and 1–3% of the foods have pesticide residue levels above the legal tolerance levels" (qtd. in Wilson and Tisdell 453). While pesticides protect the crops, humans are consuming chemicals that are intended for the killing of insects. This raises red flags for possible public health-related issues such as: acute poisoning, neurotoxicity, and cancer. Pesticides are responsible for over three million poisoning cases annually and 220,000 deaths worldwide. Persisting pesticides may linger in the environment and bioaccumulate in the food chain and result in widespread environmental contamination (Osman 205). Even though pesticides originated in one area for the purpose of protecting crops, the permanent effects are widespread. If the continual usage of pesticides on monocrop fields is allowed to persist, it is important to prevent the causes of health and environmental problems, rather than reactively treating its symptoms.

As the soil depleting characteristics of monoculture make it impractical for farmers to practice using natural means of production, farmers must use increasing amounts of artificial fertilizers in order to compensate for the loss of soil nutrients. Plants that cannot readily convert nitrogen from the atmosphere or phosphorus from sediment into nutrients, are treated with fertilizers so that they gain these nutrients that allow them to grow. Research included in *Vital Signs 1998: The Environmental Trends that are Shaping Our Future,* explains that since 1960 fertilizer use has increased from 46 million metric tonnes to about 130 million metric tonnes in 1990, this usage will need to be doubled by 2030 to maintain current crop production rates (qtd. in Ayoub 119). As the increasing institutionalization of monoculture demands ever larger quantities of chemicals, a doubling of fertilizer usage may cause damages that are readily apparent not just in future generations, but for those in this current generation. This can create a barren, lifeless land, forcing farmers to clear land in other areas to repeat the process of soil exhaustion.

When nutrient laden runoff from soil depletion is deposited into water sources, problems such as eutrophication of aquatic ecosystems can occur. Eutrophication is the build-up of nutrients in water sources, which causes the excessive growth of harmful algal blooms that coat the water surface in a green blanket (Ayoub). When the algal blooms start to breakdown down by aerobic bacteria, it creates an influx of depleted oxygen levels in the water. This process creates areas called "dead zones" in which no marine organisms can survive due to a complete lack of dissolved oxygen. The effects are so extreme that the fish that are unfortunate enough to swim through these zones die almost immediately from suffocation. This phenomenon has strongly impacted the Great Lakes, most prominently Lake Erie. Due to Erie's relatively shallow depth and warmer temperature, it is a perfect breeding ground for harmful algal blooms. In fact, "Lake Erie receives 60% of the total phosphorus and 68% of the dissolved reactive phosphorus that enters Lake Erie almost all from the Maumee River and the Detroit River" (Mitsch 407). Lake Erie, a model of excessive runoff fertilizer, exemplifies how the careless use of agricultural chemicals indirectly damages human health. Harmful algal blooms threaten Lake Erie's supply of drinking water which is consumed by over 11 million people, exclusive of its recreational and tourism industry. Additionally, certain strains of algal blooms that have been detected in Lake Erie have been labeled as irritants or suspected carcinogens after being subjected to chronic exposure of the blooms (Watson et al 46). The slow, yet steady destruction of the environment, whether it be through the augmentation of algal blooms or the desertification of farmland, threatens human health in the long term. However, while this degradation is inevitable with the current state of public involvement as low as it is, there are steps that can be taken to ensure recovery.

In order to satisfy my curiosity for sustainable alternatives to conventional farming, I decided to serve at Grand Valley State University's SAP (Sustainable Agriculture Project), a quaint and lush farm, ironically encapsulated by a large cornfield. Unfortunately, the farm hands at the SAP have immediately been impacted by the surrounding monoculture field engulfing their sustainable sanctuary. Kelly Parker, a member of the SAP's Advisory Council, spoke out about the harmful impacts that conventional farming has on the SAP. She explained that the integrity of the SAP's soil has worsened due to the influx of polluted runoff from the surrounding corn field. More intriguing, Parker expressed her ideology as to how farmers could feasibly step away from detrimental practices of monoculture and transition to sustainable, yet practical methods:

> [Farmers] see a higher potential reward with the new alternative [sustainable techniques] or they see that their present approach won't continue to be viable, whether economically or environmentally...It isn't so much that established farmers are going to change their ways, but that new farmers will bring in new ways over time.

Parker advocates not for the complete uprooting of the current agricultural system, but for the gradual shift to more natural methods of farming that, while initially more expensive, will aid the possibility of a sustainable future rather than contribute to its demise.

The SAP uses techniques that counteract the effects of intensive agriculture methods by using permaculture, cover crops, no-tillage soil, and conservative irrigation practices. These practices mimic naturally occurring processes, ensuring that the byproducts of agriculture are as ecologically efficient and responsible as possible. This means that rather than force the land to accommodate the crops through the use of chemicals, permaculture focuses on growing plants in the types of environments where they would naturally be found. By introducing greater crop diversity, permaculture works to nurture the soil rather than deplete its nutrients, cutting the demand for tilling and crop rotation. While permaculture refers to the general idea of sustainable agriculture, there are more specific techniques to combat the types of industrial farming that harm the environment and the people within it.

Cover crops, a process that is integrated by permaculture, can be seen at GVSU's SAP. The countless rows of tomatoes suspended from the ceiling of the greenhouse looked like a red and green mystical vineyard. Surrounding the ground where the tomatoes began their journey upwards were more green leafy plants. These cover crops such as parsley and rye help pull nutrients from the soil to the subsoil for the tomatoes to use. The cover crops also provide shade for the prevention of germinating weeds and negate soil erosion (Darwich and Eardley). This natural technique of warding off weeds uses only water, sunlight, and carbon dioxide rather than harmful chemicals used in monoculture. This technique "makes us stronger" according to Yumiko Jakobcic, a SAP advisor and campus sustainability coordinator. She explains that "if the SAP has a variety of crops, we may only lose a portion if a storm, pest, or disease wiped through. The variety creates a stronger wall of protection of plants rather than one large field of a single crop that is easily vulnerable." This means that in addition to reducing the use of harmful chemicals, shifting to natural methods will decrease the dependency on a singular crop and may create a source of produce that is overall more reliable.

As related to cover crops practiced by the SAP for pest control, another strategy available for reducing the nationwide dependence on monoculture is the use of integrated pest management (IPM), a sustainable technique designed to replace chemical fertilizers. A report from the Food and Agriculture Organization Panel of Experts on Integrated Pest Control defines Integrated pest management as a process that ". . . utilizes all suitable techniques and methods in as compatible a manner as possible, and maintains the pest populations at levels below those causing economically unacceptable damage or loss" (qtd. in Peshin and Pimentel 7). IPM focuses on long-term prevention of pests rather than immediate extermination. This is accomplished by utilizing biological controls such as introducing a natural enemy into the field to control pest populations (Abrol 269). Ladybugs are a prime example as they eat aphids who feed and transmit disease between different plants.

A more dramatic solution to the problems created by monoculture would be to cut all government farming subsidies. As previously mentioned, government subsidies incentivize farmers to incorporate monoculture onto their farms. Baylen Linnekin, author of "'Big Food' Bigger Thanks to 'Big Government'" shares a similar idea: "Agricultural subsidies cost taxpayers more than $15 billion each year, and until those subsidies are eliminated, farming in America will never be sustainable . . . Killing off agricultural subsidies can help ensure a sustainable future for farming in America." This progressive idea can work to cut the root of monocultures continuation. However, the cut subsidies could be distributed to smaller, multi-crop farms that will encourage and incentivize sustainable practices. While cutting all subsidies at once would surely cause many American citizens who are employed in the farming industry to lose their jobs, it could be favorable to implement subsidies to farms who practice sustainable methods. However, Parker explains that there has been very little government support for alternative methods of farming due to the societal structures dedicated to the already profitable economics of agriculture.

In order for these solutions to be implemented into conventional farming techniques, educational awareness and change in government litigation must act as the forefront for sustainable farming. Currently, large agricultural industries are only further incentivized to continually use artificial and damaging processes in pursuit of government subsidies. While these companies survive financially in the short term, they contribute to long-term environmental consequences that will eventually require far more money and resources to mediate than they do now. Luckily, these solutions are in sight of the development towards natural and sustainable farming techniques. However, these methods can only work if, following the initiative of the SAP, the people and the governments that they reside under work collectively toward a gradual shift from chemical to natural, a process with rewards far more pressing than its immediate drawbacks.

*Word Count: 2505*

Works Cited

Abrol, Dharam. *Integrated Pest Management: Current Concepts and Ecological Perspective.*Academic Press, 2017, pp. 269.

Alizamir, Saed, et al. "An Analysis of Price vs. Revenue Protection: Government Subsidies in the Agriculture Industry." *Management Science*, 2018, doi:10.1287/mnsc.2017.2927.

Ayoub, Ali T. "Fertilizers and the Environment." *Nutrient Cycling in Agroecosystems*, vol. 55, no. 2, 1999, pp. 119., doi:10.1023/a:1009808118692.

Darwich, Youseff, and Dana Eardley. "GVSU Sustainable Agriculture Project Handbook." 2015, https://www.gvsu.edu/cms4/asset/E1C67F41-C618-56D0-58AEC2992A67FB82/sap_handbook_final.pdf.

Harrison, Roy M., et al. "Environmental Impacts on Modern Agriculture." *Issues in Environmental Science and Technology*, 05 Jul. 2012 *ProQuest*, vol. 34, pp. 115.https://ebookcentral.proquest.com/lib/gvsu/detail.action?docID=1185495.

Ivey, Linda L. "Monoculture." *Encyclopedia of American Environmental History,* edited by Kathleen A. Brosnan, vol. 3, Facts on File, 2011, pp. 930. Gale Virtual Reference Library, http://link.galegroup.com.ezproxy.gvsu.edu/apps/doc/CX1981000523/GVRL?u=lom_gvalleysu&sid=GVRL&xid=6a4f58be.

Jakobcic, Yumiko. Personal interview. 31 Oct. 2018.

Linnekin, Baylen. "Big Food" Bigger Thanks to "Big Government." *Biting the Hands That Feed Us: How Fewer, Smarter Laws Would Make Our Food System More Sustainable.* Island Press, 2016.

Mitsch, William J. "Solving Lake Erie's Harmful Algal Blooms by Restoring the Great Black Swamp in Ohio." *Ecological Engineering,* vol. 108, 2017, pp. 407., doi:10.1016/j.ecoleng.2017.08.040.

Osman, Khaled A. "Pesticides and Human Health." *Pesticides in the Modern World - Effects of Pesticides Exposure,* 2011, pp. 205., doi:10.5772/16516.

Parker, Kelly. Personal interview. 2 Nov. 2018.

Peshin, Rajinder, and David Pimentel. "Integrated Pest Management." *Integrated Pest Management Pesticide Problems,* Vol. 3, Springer Netherlands, 2014, pp. 7.

Watson, Susan B., et al. "The Re-Eutrophication of Lake Erie: Harmful Algal Blooms and Hypoxia." *Harmful Algae,* vol. 56, 2016, pp. 46., doi:10.1016/j.hal.2016.04.010.

Wilson, Clevo, and Clem Tisdell. "Why Farmers Continue to Use Pesticides Despite Environmental, Health and Sustainability Costs." *Ecological Economics,* vol. 39, no. 3, 2001, pp. 453., doi:10.1016/s0921-8009(01)00238-5.

# EXEMPLARY INDIVIDUAL ESSAYS

We had 28 students nominated to submit portfolios to be considered for the *Guide to First-Year Writing At Grand Valley State University* last year. If we could, we would publish all of them, but we are limited to selecting just a handful.

For this edition, the editors decided that we wanted to include individual essays that stood out from the 84 student essays we read and discussed this year. These nine essays were exemplary models of student writing, and we loved reading them, so we wanted you to read them, too.

# A GIFT FROM A BUTTERFLY

### Amberly Dzimira

Amberly Dzimira, an Advertising and Public relations major with a minor in Mangagement, says she learned a good deal in her first-year writing course. A native of Romeoville, Illinois, Amberly believes that her work in Professor Jim Van Sickle's course "changed the way [she] view[s] writing." She explains, "I will always read my work in the future as if I had the mind of an audience member. I now understand that sometimes what makes sense to me will not always make sense to the reader."

I found myself in a trance, slowly stumbling down the carpeted hallways and into the bathroom, shutting the door quickly behind me. The motion sensor lights flickered on, I stood in front of the mirror staring back at myself with disbelief. My mouth hung open, gasping for air. My eyes felt like they were stung by a swarm of bees. I gripped the sides of the sink, my knees shook, wanting desperately to release the newly added weight from my heart, causing me to crash to the cold, tiled floor. My body felt as if I just jumped into a freezing cold lake and my heart pounded so loudly, I was confident the hungry residents a few feet from the door could hear it perfectly. Without the time to process the painful news I received just seconds earlier, I tucked my blue work shirt into my black pants, adjusted my apron, and looked in the mirror one last time before walking out to begin my five-hour shift.

April 30, 2017, I tucked in that same blue shirt, although much fresher, into my black pants for the first time. It was my first day of work, and I was anxious. Although two years ago, I can still remember my first steps in the doors of Senior Star, the local nursing home just five minutes from my house. The sliding doors swung open; I was looking into a large lobby filled with several beige couches accompanied by elders reading books by the tall floor lamps which provided a warm, and comforting light. Despite it being a nursing home, the atmosphere was strangely comforting. On my left, there was another room labeled "Weber Pub" where a bar, TV, and more couches occupied the space. To my right, there was a desk with an employee talking on the phone. With a lack of direction, I studied the floor map which was placed on the wall, tapping my right foot repeatedly. I began wandering the long, blue carpeted halls for what felt like forever before I found the dining room, my new area of work. The dining room was beautiful, it had high ceilings decorated with ivy vines swinging from wall to wall. Two walls were a beautiful, fresh shade of white, and the others were covered in blue floral wallpaper. The center of the dining room held a large amount of small, circular tables. They were a lovely white wood, white chairs with blue cushions for comfort were pushed into them, awaiting to be used. Gazing at the massive amount of seating, it was quite intimidating to imagine all of them filled with hungry residents. The room was brightly lit due to the sun shining through the large windows. At the back of the room, I saw a blonde-haired girl waving at me, her hair shining vibrantly from the bright sun.

"Hi! I am Eliana, I will be training you today." She had a low-pitched voice which displayed authority and assertiveness. She wore the same serving outfit that I out on for the first time that day, yet her shirt was faded and worn in. For an hour I was Eliana's apprentice. I followed her around the dining room as she explained how my new serving job worked. She showed me the section I would be serving and gave me a tour of the kitchen and introduced me to my new coworkers. Towards the end of the training shift, Eliana offered me some advice: "If you get attached easily, I would try your best not to make close connections with the residents here. It makes it less painful when they pass." Eliana's advice seemed selfish, but for my first month at Senior Star I decided to follow it. I was friendly to everyone, yet I held myself back from making connections with the residents in order to protect my own well-being. That all changed when I met a man named Ed Krall.

Ed Krall never seemed to have a bad day. He was noticeably a happy man; he always had a big smile on his face and wore brightly colored sweaters in the shades purple, orange, pink, and his favorite, blue. Sitting in my section, every evening I had the honor of serving him. Ed would come in around 4pm and have apple juice with ice, whatever the dinner special was, and a piece of dessert with hot tea. He ate this every single day and never complained once. Although he was an intriguing man, I never intended to get close to Ed, until he spoke to me one day.

"Hey, you!" he shouted as I walked around my section.

"Me?" I responded with utter confusion.

"Yes you, come sit and talk to me for one moment." I listened to the man in the pink sweater who was drinking steaming hot tea and sat down in the chair across from him. He looked at me for a second before revealing what was on his mind.

"You remind me of my daughter when she was your age, you look exactly like her. She spent a lot of her time working as well, except she worked at a grocery store. She spent so much time slouched over while stocking shelves, she ended up with scoliosis."

"How old is your daughter now?" I responded out of curiosity.

"She is in her 60s, she is getting to be an old woman now. It truly is crazy how fast life goes when you have so much fun living in it. She is one of my four children, I have thirteen grandchildren and eight greatgrandchildren, it is amazing. Family is a beautiful thing; I hope one day you get to raise a big family of your own. Next time my daughter is here I will introduce you to her."

Following that first conversation with Ed, a bond was formed between us. Knowing I was able to sit down when no work needed to be done, Ed began staying late everyday waiting patiently for my other tables to leave before ordering his dessert. I would sit with him and drink hot tea with him as he ate his dessert. I listened to his stories of war, love, and family. I asked questions about his life and as a result I learned so much about him throughout the months of our teatime. He made many jokes, his laugh was contagious. While listening to his stories, I always doodled pictures on the sticky notes I carried in my apron. I gave all my drawings to Ed; his favorite were butterflies. I never asked why he loved butterflies so much, but I made sure to draw him plenty.

Senior Star hosted parties every month to provide the residents fun and give them the opportunity to invite their family for some quality time. Hosted in the dining room, the high ceilings were decorated extravagantly with colorful flowers and ribbons. A band was hired for each event, making the dining room come alive with the beautiful instruments, singing, and dancing. Ed especially loved to dance. Although 94 years old with a frail figure and a weak hip, he never stopped dancing. It was clear to see there was a young spirit trapped within Ed's heart. He radiated happiness wherever he went, he gained many friends at Senior Star and was loved by so many. With all the love he had, he enjoyed every moment of life he could. The dances Senior Star hosted brought Ed and I even closer as friends. I danced with Ed at every party. Every single one. I met many members of his family, including the daughter that sparked our friendship. She had my bright green eyes and dimples on both cheeks. Ed and his family were always kind to me, they treated me like one of their own.

September 13, 2017, I worked a dinner shift, but as always, I was excited for it. I enjoyed going to work and spending my time with Ed, our teatime tradition was important to me. Walking through the sliding doors, I sensed a different atmosphere than the one I knew. The halls were empty, the once lively dining room was dull, I was able to hear my every step while walking through the room. My coworkers stared at me as I entered the kitchen but looked away once I met their gaze. I instantly knew something was wrong, but my throat clenched up as if I had not had a sip of water in days, leaving me unable to question them. I made my way into the dining room and stood in my section, tapping my right foot. It was well past 4, my section was filled, but Ed's chair remained empty. Brushing my coworkers stares away, I decided not to panic. There were plenty of times where Ed missed dinner to spend time with family, or maybe he was sick, or maybe he was just running late, or maybe the elevator was stuck. My mind raced with ideas, but they were soon put to rest once I heard a conversation from two ladies who sat in my section.

"Did you hear what happened to Ed?" The lady with gray curls asked her friend.

"Yes, I did. Dead in his sleep, at least he went peacefully" responded the second lady who wore bright pink lipstick. A sharp pain appeared in my stomach; my heart dropped as if I was stuck on a roller coaster. Without thinking, I stumbled through the now dimmed dining room making my way to the bathroom thinking I was going to be sick. Grasping the sides of the bathroom sink, I stared at my somber reflection. My apron began to suffocate me, I struggled to untie it, trying desperately to breathe. I closed my eyes, trapping the tears behind my heavy eyelids. I had no time to cry. I had no time to fully react to the situation. I had to work. Tucking in my shirt and retying my apron, I left the bathroom and reentered the dull dining room, feeling like a minnow swimming into shark infested waters.

The starved residents in my section turned to stare at me with angered expressions, I stared back with a blank gaze. I hurried into the kitchen to start my duties. My body was trembling, my heart was beating so loud I could hardly hear the orders being spitted at me. I wanted so desperately to be in my bed at home, with the covers over my head shielding me from this nightmare. Although normally able to hold my tray with one hand, that day I held it firmly with two. My hands shook profusely as I tried pouring coffee, and I continuously forgot residents' orders, unable to shake away what was truly on my mind. Elina was right, I was a fool to go against her advice and to make a connection with someone here. I was heartbroken. This place which I once glorified abruptly turned into a place I never wanted to step foot in again. The walls were no longer a shining white; the wallpaper was peeling from them desperately trying to escape. The blue carpeting was suddenly gray and filthy, completely worn out from constantly being trampled on. After poorly completing my shift that night, I did not return for a week.

Whenever a resident passes, the family has a choice to host a memorial service at Senior Star, giving the option for the friends of the resident and the workers who served them to pay their respect. I returned to Senior Star to attend Ed's memorial service. Held in the Weber Pub, the room was filled with Ed's family, friends, fellow residents, and employees dressed in their finest clothes; pictures of Ed were on every wall. Looking around the room, my eyes met with my coworkers', they smiled and waved. I returned a quick smile but turned away quickly to look at a picture of Ed, knowing if I spoke to someone I would break down. The picture on the wall was recently taken, it showed Ed smiling brightly to the camera, with a small child sitting comfortably on his lap. He wore his favorite blue sweater. Staring at the picture, sadness slithered through my body like a snake. I wondered if his family knew how good of a dancer he was, how happy butterflies made him, and how much he loved his hot tea and dessert. I was sure that many of his grandchildren and greatgrandchildren never had the chance to dance with him, or even have many in depth conversations with him.

In effort to destroy the sad thoughts that were trying effortlessly to conquer my mind, I continued to walk around the crowded room, looking for distractions. A board at the back of the room caught my eye. As I made my way to it, suddenly everyone in the room disappeared and I was alone at the memorial service, frozen to the floor in amazement. I could not believe what was in front of me. Butterflies. The board was covered in various post it notes colors of pink, purple, yellow, and blue. My post it notes, with my scribbles of butterflies. Ed kept every drawing I gave him for months. I stood in front of the board incapable of moving when I felt a hand on my weak shoulder and heard a familiar voice.

"He really loved you, he talked about you often. You gave him the time to talk and share his life experiences and many people here do not do that when they should. You were a main reason why he was happy until the day he died, even living in a nursing home." I recognized the man next to me, it was Ed's youngest son who I met at one of the parties. As if I had no tongue, I simply smiled and nodded, but his son continued speaking to me.

"Thank you. Thank you for being so kind to him. We put these up for you, we found them in one of his drawers. He really did love butterflies, he always told me he believed they represented family. Ed thought of you as family." With this, the only thing I could manage to do to show my appreciation was to hug the man. Resting my face onto the man's chest, I smiled, finally feeling the weight being lifted off my shoulders.

There were no tears shed at Ed's memorial service. Instead of spending the time mourning, his family shared happy memories with Ed and their favorite things about him. I pitched in, talking about our teatime traditions and how happy he looked when he was dancing. We laughed instead of cried, we comforted one another, we celebrated his life instead of letting his light die out. Regardless if we were blood related or not, that day we were all family. It was beautiful.

I returned to work the next day. Walking back into the brightly lit dining room, my heart was warmed from what I saw. I missed the high ceilings, blue carpeting, and the smiling faces of the resident sitting at their wooden tables. Looking around, I saw a new face sitting where Ed used to. Taking a deep breath, I walked towards the woman. She was frail, with a purple walker to her left side of her chair. She wore large, thick glasses that covered half of her face and a purple sweatshirt paired with olive-green pants. I smiled at her, and she smiled back.

"Hi, my name is Amberly, I serve this section. It is so nice to meet you. What is your name?"

"Marie" she responded in a hoarse voice. "I'm sorry if this is the wrong place for me to sit, I am new here and I don't know how anything works!" She reached for the glass of water sitting in front of her, her hands shook profusely. Marie continued to tell me about her experience moving in and how sad she felt when her family left.

After my shift that night I went to Marie's room which was cluttered with small, brown boxes in every corner. I helped her unpack some of her belongings. I hung up picture frames of her family, gazing at the pictures of young Marie, learning about her life through the images that stared back at me. Sitting on her soft couch, Marie and I talked for two hours before I said goodnight and left. I was no longer afraid to make connections anymore. Driving home from work that night, I was the happiest I've been in a long time. No longer did I fear making connections.

Ed has had the biggest impact on my life. He continues to be my role model. I aspire to be as happy as he was throughout his entire life. Losing Ed was one of the most heartbreaking things to have ever happened to me, and for a long time, I believed I lost my passion for my job. I was terrified to open myself up to another person that I knew I could lose at any moment. After Ed's memorial service I realized making connections with anyone is one of the most important things a person can do, regardless of how old they are. I made Ed's last moments of life more enjoyable, and that makes me extremely happy. As of right now, making connections with the residents at work is my top priority. Showing interest to someone's life and giving them time reflect upon it will make their day, I guarantee it. Especially with those who are older and more experienced with life; they are walking textbooks. Since Ed's death, I now aspire to one day be an executive director of a nursing home, bringing my personal experiences with me. Instead of telling those to be cautious of making connections, I plan to strongly encourage it. My connection with Ed will always be my favorite; he has taught me so much that I never knew I needed to learn. He will forever be my butterfly.

*Word Count: 3023*

# POP

### Madison Carmichael

Madison Carmichael is a nursing major from Saginaw, Michigan. As a student Professor Aiman Mueller's class, she was challenged by the "trial and error" of writing and revising her essays, but because she had a mindset that "there is always room for improvement," her hard work paid off. Her advice to you: "Take full advantage of the course. This course will give you information you will use your entire lives, and will allow you to explore your ideas through your essays."

As I was driving down a country road one night I could see the flashes of light coming from my iPhone alerting me of texts I was receiving. The texts came from my usual list of people I spent my days with, along with a text from my best friend, my mom. I was pondering the endless options of prom dresses I was going to choose from for the dance coming up. My mom wanted the gold dress, my boyfriend wanted the black, and I wanted the pink. At the time, the kind of dress I wanted was one of the only worries in my life.

That particular night the texts were pouring in. This caused me to get an itch to see what was going on. I unlocked my phone to see my mom sent me a video of my bunny eating carrots followed by more mindless texts from my friends. As I started to respond I felt my car start to hover over the outline of the street and onto the gravel until it turned into grass. The texting distracted me to the point where I underestimated how far my car was drifting off the path. As I lifted my head and went to jerk my wheel back to the center of the lane, I was met with the sight of a 4-foot-wide tree.

It was too late to regain my blissful state of driving down the road.

The sight of this 20-foot tall tree caused my body to completely shut down. The air in my lungs seemed to escape before I could take another breath. The only thing that seemed to function was my foot plunging into the brake pedal as hard as it could.

All of my senses became numb in that moment and my world turned into slow motion. It was all happening so fast yet it in my mind it felt like minutes. My ears went silent from the world and tuned into soft ringing that seemed to echo through my entire body.

It felt as if black paint was being poured down my eyes, slowly dripping over my entire pupil so that I was blinded. It was like God wanted to save me from the horrific sight that was about to take place.

The moment after the crash it took me a second to move the airbags out of my face and realize what just happened. My whole body ached. It felt like my bones were rusty and I needed some sort of oil to allow them to move efficiently. The sensation in my body was numb, almost like my body wasn't there. I opened the door and felt the cold air on my face as I fell onto the middle of the right lane. Once I was able to take in the sight of my mangled car I brought my dirtied hands to my eyes and searched for blood. I saw the glow of a headlight brighten up the red stream running down my hand. I have never been so happy to see the headlights of a car coming towards me in the opposite lane.

I felt a sensation of comfort spread through my body. I started to thank God that somebody was coming my way. My arms waved frantically as I screamed in both shock and relief. Soon the truck was only a couple feet before me. I watched helplessly as the truck sped past the sight of my car wrapped around the tree while I was lying next to it. The dust from the truck speeding past my body engulfed me.

*I'm in the middle of the street, didn't he see me?*

The trucks lights forced me to become disoriented. I was clueless to who drove past me, but I knew I hated them. I hated them for being unaware of my pain and fear, for disregarding how I felt and carrying on with their own life. This made my blood boil, shifting my body temperature from a feeling of ice to a burning fire in a matter of seconds.

*Oblivious.*

Fear was once again weighing down on my heart. In that moment the feeling of loneliness was painfully something I couldn't ignore. I was laying there alone on the cold concrete, forced to face the reality that I was now under the category of people in which horrible things happened to. This was my wake-up call.

\* \* \*

Things like unexpected deaths or tragedy wasn't something that was prominent in my life. My parents spent hours watching the news stories that came on TV. I'd walk past the TV with my pink headphones in, scrolling through Twitter and Instagram. I was a materialistic girl who hadn't had the slightest clue what was going on in the world. My mentality consisted of the saying, "Whatever it is, it isn't happening to me."

When I later recalled the moment the truck passed me I had an epiphany. I was just like that person in the car; an ignorant, self-absorbed person. Remembering when they passed me used to make me feel resentment, but I started to realize that before this accident happened to me, I would have been that person passing another person in need.

*Who was I to call this person oblivious?*

The blinding white light of the truck's headlights removed my innocence all at once. The moment the beaming light hit my eyes felt like walking through a dark parking lot late at night when all at once, every street light illuminates the space around. Before the lights came on, my vision was dim and lacked full awareness. In both of these moments, I was unaware that I needed light to see more vividly, but once the lights were on, I would never see the same again.

My car accident forced my life to flip up-side down. Sadness and pain became a much wider, more prominent section in my every day thoughts. I became painfully away that life was not a constant state of happiness.

My mom and I sat in my hospital bed and cried tears of laughter after the accident.

Although I felt lucky to be alive, I soon became more aware of the life that went on around me. Weeks after, I began to lose the euphoria I felt from surviving. I slowly started to make the transition from the fantasy world I seemed to be living in to the reality that life had some of the greatest tragedies I will ever encounter.

After my recovery, I started to tune into the things happening around me. The Fort Lauderdale Airport had an armed man shooting people dead. Hurricane Irma and Harvey were swallowing people's homes and lives. A terrorist set off an explosive device at an Ariana Grande concert. A psychopath took an automatic weapon and shot after thousands of people dancing to country music.

*When did all of this start happening? Or maybe I should ask when I started truly observing life around me.*

*Had life always been this way?*

I was in my own personal security bubble up until my accident. The crash took my bubble and popped it.

A couple months after the incident I remember walking through a highly populated area. Instead of enjoying people-watching like I would usually do, anxiety slowly creeped into my stomach and set-up camp. A thought popped into my head:

*What's stopping a terrorist from targeting this area, and the people standing around me? Terrorists thrive off happy gatherings with thousands of people.*

These kinds of thoughts eventually become constant. Things that used to bring me happiness like going to a concert or flying on an airplane raises a red flag in my mind, making me uneasy for a moment. The moment will usually pass, but not until I go through every possible bad outcome of the situation.

*My assigned seat is far enough back on the plane so that if the plane nose dives I have a higher chance of survival. If the plane is blown-up in the air, there's a chance we'll be flying over the ocean and our fall will be met with water. I can swim.*

As a kid, flying made me feel invincible. Now, it's a little darker and more frightening.

As a year went by since the accident my dreams no longer consisted of light-hearted nonsense. Even sleep did not relieve me of reality. The nightmares started to become real-life situations that I subconsciously feared. Nightmares about being held at gunpoint or falling out of a 20-foot story building because of a terrorist attack isn't something that I find out of the ordinary now. My bed used to be my safe zone, but now it seems to be another place to harbor my fears. There was a constant reminder that life was something to fear as well as befriend.

*Is there any way to reverse this?*

To this day, my accident causes my mind to operate differently. I never fully understood the saying "ignorance is bliss" until my accident. Now I understand that life feels lighter when the bad is unknown. The bliss is like a person floating on top of the ocean while there is a shark beneath them. They are unbothered and fearless because they are simply unaware of the situation. I was once this person.

Was this my crossover from childhood to adulthood? Children possess an incredible innocence that allows their life to be simple. My 10-year old imagination allowed me to enjoy the warm sun on my face or the feel of the ocean water between my toes. My newly founded adult mind will remind me that I could die of skin cancer without sunscreen, or that I should really wear water shoes to protect my feet from possible biting crabs.

Today I called my mom for what seemed like the 100th time this month. We discussed how each other's day was going and then she asked me if I chose the dress I wanted to wear to my formal dance.

I said, "Did you hear about the 19-year old that shot 17 helpless children in the Parkland Highschool today?"

*Word Count: 1691*

# AN INTOXICATING TRUTH

## Anna Patton

For Anna Patton, a Psychology and Public and Nonprofit Administration double major from Troy, Michigan, her writing course gave her an opportunity to write about topics that matter to her. She explains, "My favorite part of writing these essays in Professor Teresa Gibbons' class was the reflection…Research was crucial in each essay, but one of the best parts was connecting my research to my personal experience. Reflecting on my own experience provided me the opportunity to fully engage with each of my essay topics."

February 24th, 2018, at 1:26 am a missed call notification illuminated my bedroom, and the voice mail from my best friend blurted out, "Please pick up. Elli fell. She is headed to the hospital." The next morning at school, my friend approached me with tears in her eyes and explained how lucky I was that I had left the party early. The night before, my friend, Elli, had thrown a party at her house, something she did every weekend, because her parents traveled often for work. Over a hundred students would usually cram into her house, and alcohol was always provided plentifully by students' older siblings. That night, Elli was waving goodbye to our friends when she called out from her window and fell face first, eleven feet down, onto an icy concrete slab. My best friend drove intoxicated to the emergency room with a very drunk Elli pooling blood in the back of her car. Parties were frequent at my high school, yet no one thought of the horrific consequences that could come with them.

Two months later, dressed in ball gowns, my friends and I received the news that Elli's heart had stopped the night of our senior prom. She had undergone four brain surgeries, and her body could not handle anymore. After her first surgery surgeons informed us if Elli were to survive, she would have little cognitive ability. After prom, blame swept my school as students pointed fingers. My best friend blamed herself, because she had dragged Elli out of her car the night of the accident. She abandoned her outside the doors of the emergency room and left her bleeding out in front of the hospital for close to forty-five minutes before a nurse found her. When found, Elli was identified by her phone, and her parents were contacted immediately. My friend who left her at the hospital would soon face interrogations by the police for allegations of murder. The doctors later educated my school at an assembly that if 911 would have been called immediately Elli may have survived and the criminal case would not have happened. The night of the accident my friend was concerned that if she was caught drinking, she would lose her full ride to college due to a contract the majority of scholarships make students sign. No one at my high school had been educated on what to do in an emergency situation, and they were fearful that calling 911 would result in a misdemeanor as a minor in possession. Since underage binge drinking is impossible to prevent, every state should be required to have proper drinking education, programs that include resources and education on what to do in a crisis; also, legislation should be modified to provide the safest situations for the youth of America.

*New York Times* Notable Author, Emily Listfield explained in the article "Binge Drinking Is a Serious Problem for Underage Drinkers," that when adults partake in drinking it typically is meant for a social or casual setting, while unlike underage drinking, ninety percent of the time the end goal is to achieve drunkenness. Many high schoolers are under extreme societal pressures to perform well in school and be involved in numerous activities and sports. To alleviate the anxiety many teens are facing, they turn to extreme alcohol consumption, which many times falls in line with many alcoholic tendencies. In party settings it is easier for teens to interact under the influence, because they are less conscious of their actions. Francis M. Harding, an employee of the Substance Abuse and Mental Health Services Administration, conducted a study finding 25.7% of tenth-graders reported the consumption of alcohol in the past thirty days. When I was a sophomore in high school, peers of mine threw a party that the cops shut down and issued twenty-three minor in possessions with breathalyzers blowing almost three times above the legal driving limit. This was the first of many incidents that occurred in my grade involving binge drinking, yet the school district and many parents seemed to turn their backs to the issue. When some concerned parents reached out to the school, the administration explained the incident was not the school's matter to handle.

Graduation requirements for my high school had a requisite that every student partake in a semester of a health-related course.

Through the State of Michigan, it is stated in the Michigan Merit Curriculum for High School Graduation Requirements, that every student must take 1 credit of a health course in high school (Michigan Department of Education). Every school district varies in required curriculum; in my class, drinking and drugs were combined in lessons on abstinence and were taught as things to avoid. We learned statistics on the medical risks of drinking such as liver cancer and drunk driving accidents among adults. My teacher preached that drinking is a bad decision, and no resources were given for when a drinking accident does occur. One thing that could have potentially saved Elli's life was getting her immediate medical attention, yet students lacked the knowledge of medical amnesty. From the State of Michigan, the enrolled house bill No. 4393, put into effect in June 2012, implemented that any minor who has consumed alcohol and needs medical attention or is with another minor during an emergency will not be legally penalized (State of Michigan). This education is crucial, and the bill should be required information in every high school health course curriculum. With the high amount of high school binge drinkers, the probability of an accident or alcohol poisoning occurring is likely. With medical amnesty the person calling for or receiving medical attention will not be punished. Additionally, it was found in a research study that alcohol is the cause of death for more than 4,300 youths annually (Harding). With the high rate of mortality in youths due to drinking accidents, any preventative information should be taught to students. It can be argued that medical amnesty enables minors to drink alcohol, yet unless there is a medical emergency the same protocol is set for disciplinary action.

Elli's accident and the toll her loss took on my peers could have been easily prevented by something as simple as knowledge. The Centers for Disease Control and Prevention released data that in 2013 the emergency rooms visited for injuries and health problems linked to alcohol for those ages 12 to 21 was approximately 119,000 times ("Underage Drinking"). In a perfect world, minors would not be able to get access to alcohol, but with beverages being easily accessible, it is not uncommon for students to partake in risky behavior. With the frequent amount of hospital visits it leads to costly medical bills, and the patients take up a doctor's time that could be spent helping others. High school health course curriculum should encompass medical amnesty, and additional information on binge drinking. Education should include the signs and symptoms of alcohol poisoning, and how to assist someone when they are heavily intoxicated. Adolescents are going to consume alcohol regardless of if a high school teacher tells them to abstain from it. High schools have the influence to readily prepare students for crisis situations that may arise. My high school conducted assemblies that educated us on smart drinking choices, and how to help someone in drinking emergencies. This information was not taught to my school until after Elli's death. Every high school should prepare students before their school experiences a major trauma. Having speakers and creating a safe place to discuss alcohol safety in high schools could prevent more accidents from occurring.

Medical amnesty was not the only major component of drinking education that was lacking in my high school health curriculum. When alcohol was mentioned in class, nothing was said about the increasing problem of sexual assault that correlates with it. At the University of Georgia, Psychology Clinic Director, Emily Mouilso conducted a study and found, thirty-one percent of females said they had been sexually assaulted during their first year of college when participating in weekly binge drinking. With the likelihood of sexual assault occurring when binge drinking takes place, schools should be providing additional resources. Telling students to abstain from alcohol has not been effective, but giving resources on what to do if a sexual assault occurs would benefit numerous adolescents. I know a few of my peers experienced sexual assaults at a party setting in high school yet chose not to report it until years later due to a fear that they would be scrutinized for consuming alcohol. It is important to educate students about the time limit of a rape kit and that it is okay to speak up, because they will not be punished if alcohol was present. Binge drinking can lead to many tragic events ranging from death, severe injuries, or even sexual assault, and it is crucial that we prepare our youth on how to handle these situations when they arise.

Underage drinking is an epidemic that is affecting minors physically, emotionally, and mentally. When my community lost Elli, many of my peers, including myself had to receive counseling for issues such as post-traumatic stress disorder or extreme grief. At a young age many of my friends had to witness one of their loved ones pass away, leaving many to blame themselves. Suicidal ideation crept into many of my friends' minds, and the trauma took a very real physical toll on many close to me. Trauma exposure led many of my friends to drinking more to cope with the emotional destress they were experiencing. Lamya Khoury, the head of Psychiatry and Behavioral Sciences at Emory University of Medicine, found in a study that 70 percent of adolescent patients receiving care for substance abuse had been exposed to a serious trauma. The trauma my school experienced led many of my friends down dark paths and substance abuse became a great concern for my community. If Elli's accident had been prevented, many of my peers may not have developed substance dependence issues. The school's lack of preventative measures not only cost Elli's life, but it also led more students to possible alcoholism leading to a greater risk of more accidents potentially occurring.

The traditional health education curriculum is outdated and the need for alcohol prevention resources is a growing concern. After Elli's death my grade was informed of tools such as medical amnesty and safe drinking tactics. These vital resources can help prevent death, severe injuries, and sexual assault. It is heart breaking that someone's life had to be taken to start making changes. Abstinence is not the cure to the rising epidemic of underage binge drinking, educating and having resources available for students, can reduce the number of adolescents affected by the dangers of alcohol.

*Word Count: 1793*

Works Cited

Harding, Frances, et al. "Underage Drinking: A Review of Trends and Prevention Strategies." *American Journal of Preventive Medicine*, vol. 51, no. 4, Oct. 2016, pp. 148–157. *ScienceDirect*, https://www.sciencedirect.com/science/article/pii/S0749379716301921

Khoury, Lamya, et al. "Substance Use, Childhood Traumatic Experience, and Posttraumatic Stress Disorder in an Urban Civilian Population." *Wiley Depression and Anxiety,* Dec. 2010. *US National Library of Medicine National Institutes of Health,* https://www.ncbi.nlm.nih.gov/pmc/articles/PMC3051362/

Listfield, Emily. "Binge Drinking Is a Serious Problem for Underage Drinkers." *Alcohol Abuse,* Greenhaven Press, Opposing Viewpoints in Context, 2012. Gale, Cengage Learning, http://go.galegroup.com/ps/i.do?p=OVIC&u=lom_gvalleysu&id=GALE%7CEJ3010276239&v=2.1&it=r&sid=summon Accessed 12 Mar. 2019.

Michigan, Department of Education, *The Revised School Code (Excerpt) Act 451 of 1976.* 24 Dec. 2018, http://www.legislature.mi.gov/(hzka3q2cfmj4r0vc4mdmp055)/documents/mcl/pdf/mcl-380-1278b.pdf?20151124150842

Mouilso, Emily, et al. "A Prospective Study of Sexual Assault and Alcohol Use Among First-Year College Women." *Violence and Victmis*, vol. 27, no. 1, pp. 78–94, *ProQuest*, 2012 https://search.proquest.com/docview/921332559?pq-origsite=summon Accessed 15 Mar. 2019.

State of Michigan 96th Legislature. *Enrolled House Bill No. 4393*, 1 June 2012 https://docs.wixstatic.com/ugd/a0b749_a6ca0b2a6ffd4a789f9434bebe8a87bb.pdf

"Underage Drinking." *Centers for Disease Control and Prevention, Alcohol and Public Health,* 2 Aug. 2018 https://www.cdc.gov/alcohol/fact-sheets/underage-drinking.htm

# EUGENICS OF THE 21ST CENTURY

## Dana Williams

Dana Williams is a Public and Nonprofit Administration major with minors in Political Science and Environmental and Sustainability Studies. Dana got the idea to write about eugenics for Professor Tamara Lubic's class from a human rights course she had just completed, and this assignment gave her the opportunity to dive deeper into a topic she wanted to learn more about. She explains, "I'm proud of this essay because it comes from a place of advocacy. Eugenics wasn't something I knew a lot about initially, so I become more educated throughout the process of writing this paper."

Typically, the topic of eugenics is a thing many think of in a historical context. Thoughts of the horror stories we have heard of concentration camps built for the sole purpose of killing off a "type" of person based on attributes such as their race, ethnicity, sex, disabilities, or sexual orientation may come to mind. We think of how people can easily become separated from propaganda stating that one "type" of person is superior to another, such as the Rwandan genocide, or the Holocaust. What we do not think of is a modern day case of eugenics. However, eugenics is occurring in today's more often than talked about. It does not take on the same form as the concentration camps of the past; however, people, specifically women, are being forcibly sterilized based on race and class, as a form of modern eugenics. In the journal *Public Health News*, discrimination against women happens through these forced sterilizations in medical environments with the consent of the woman from situations of high stress, consent under false pretenses, or no consent at all (Patel 2). These three practices combined constitute sterilization as a form of eugenics and discrimination on the basis of racism, sexism, and classism.

Eugenics is defined as "the practice or advocacy of controlled selective breeding of human populations (as by sterilization) to improve the population's genetic composition" ("Eugenics"). The word and definition may be associated with Hitler, but the idea of eugenics has a long and controversial history, even in the United States. Eugenics, which comes from the Greek roots "good" and "origin", took place in the United States in the early 1900s. It was believed that negative traits could be removed from society by sterilizing those with undesirable traits, in order to stop them from being passed on. It should not come as a shock that these undesirable traits were considered minority groups, the uneducated, and the poor. Dr. Laura Rivard of San Diego University put the early eugenics movement into a historical perspective, stating that the movement started with the sterilization law in Indiana in 1907, and eugenics spread to California and twenty-eight other states and became widely accepted. Much like then, sterilizations today happen medically. In these procedures, a hysterectomy or tubal ligation is performed. These operations can be to done to consenting, well-informed women who seek the sterilization, but in several countries, they are used to forcibly or coercively sterilize women.

Priti Patel, the author of "Forced Sterilization of Women as Discrimination" makes the claim that in the cases of forced sterilization, medical professionals often coerce women to sign the consent form in moments of high stress and confusion (2). In a study to explore how deeply women with HIV are affected by forced sterilization, a woman from Mexico explained "[Medical personnel] told me that because of my HIV problem, I couldn't refuse [sterilization]" (Albert). This is just one example of the 28% of women in Mexico who were pressured to sterilize post diagnosis of HIV (Albert). The same study goes deeply into the stories of the women in Nicaragua. For example, women with HIV are sterilized under the pretext that they cannot have children and if they do not get sterilized, they will only hurt themselves or their potential children (Albert). These sterilizations often take place in the medical environment, and great stress is put on each patient. In a study about this epidemic, one mother of two from Nicaragua said, "Maybe they didn't force me, but by not giving me any options and information, I was obliged to be sterilized. If they had given me the correct information, I wouldn't have accepted sterilization," (Albert). HIV does not make a woman infertile, but without this information, a woman who believes her health is at risk would sign over her consent to be sterilized under pressure and coercion. It should also be noted that men also have HIV, and make up much more of the population of people living with HIV in Nicaragua. In the most recent study of men and women living with HIV in Nicaragua conducted in 2007, it was found that there are estimated to be over 6,000 men aged fifteen and older living with HIV, while women aged 15 and older are estimated to have 2,900 ("Nicaragua"). While men are heavily affected by this epidemic, they are not being targeted in the same way as women. In spite of the stated goal of this forced sterilization program to stop the spread of HIV, only women are being affected, demonstrating that this practice is sexist.

The second way forced sterilization happens, according to Patel, is through invalid consent. Women will be given the papers, but not completely told what they contain; therefore, giving consent on paper but not with full understanding (2). In an article documenting women's stories of forced sterilization in Peru, a woman named Clotilde was told, "You can't go on having children like animals! You have to have your tubes tied. It's a new law..." by a nurse (Olivera 31). While this was not a law at the time, the threat of being thrown in jail for refusing sterilization was very real. Peru's president, Alberto Fujimori, set these sterilizations in place as an anti-poverty reform program. *The New Republic* states that new stories of forced sterilization have emerged as early as 2013 and nearly 200,000 women were sterilized since Fujimori's political party has been in power (Kovarik). These women have not received justice or any form of compensation. In this case, many women were sterilized under the false pretense that they would be incarcerated for refusing the surgery, simply for their individual socioeconomic standing. This is a blatant example of eugenics being used to conform to a classist agenda.

Finally, Patel states the last form of forced sterilization is done without the women's consent (2). In these cases, women were not informed or asked if they wanted to be sterilized, and do not find out about the procedure until long after. This is often the case with Romani women in the Czech Republic. Historically, Roma people have been victims of several human rights violations, so it should not be surprising that they are victims of eugenics as well. In *The Health and Human Rights* journal, it is stated that from 1972 to 1990, 36 percent of sterilization in Czechoslovakia were Romani women. This is cause for concern because Romani women only make up about 2 percent of Czechoslovakia's population (Szilvasi). While these sterilizations were allegedly justified under the context that the sterilizations were for the woman's health, there have been many cases of women not giving their consent to be sterilized. While there is not a firm statistic about sterilization of Romani women in recent years, nearly one thousand Romani women have stepped up and shared their stories about coercive or forced sterilization. However, *The Health and Human Rights* journal believes that many women do not speak out on their experiences because of the negative stigma infertile women have in their culture (Szilvasi). This is eugenics based on these women's ethnicity and is a clear example of sterilization being used in acts of racism.

As recently as last year, women in Japan were fighting to be compensated for the sterilizations they were forced to undergo as late as 1998 (Hasegawa). In this case, these women were targeted based on their mental and physical disabilities. In an article sharing these women's stories and the fight for justice, it stated that it was ruled that the victims would not be receiving compensation because the procedure was legal at this time (Hasegawa). There have also been cases of unwanted sterilization to women with women diagnosed with mental and physical disabilities, transgender individuals, indigenous women, along with many others. Whether these unwanted sterilizations take place in Nicaragua or Japan, the overarching theme in these methods of sterilization and eugenics is that women are being marginalized and put in a vulnerable position to be forcibly or coercively sterilized, with or without consent. This is an outright human rights violation and should be enforced more than it currently is. However, because eugenics is more commonly thought of in a historical context, it does not get the deserved public discourse and media converage it should. It will take more cultural awareness for this issue to come to light and be enforced. In terms of human rights measures, the United Nations Universal Declaration of Human Rights, the Committee on the Elimination of Discrimination Against Women, and the Convention on the Prevention and Punishment of the Crime of Genocide address forced sterilization as a human rights violation, a crime against women, and a form of genocide. If these measures were enforced in countries with accusations or proof of forced sterilization, this practice would not be as commonplace as it is today. At present, however, women of different races in poor communities are being taken advantage of in a system of eugenics that works on the basis of forced or coerced sterilization. This sterilization can be obtained through consent in moments of duress, consent under false pretenses, and no consent at all.

*Word Count: 1521*

Works Cited

Albert, Claire. "Experiences of Coercion to Sterilize and Forced Sterilization among Women Living with HIV in Latin America." *Journal of the International AIDS Society*, vol. 18, no. 1, Jan. 2015, p. 1–N.PAG. *Academic Search Premier*, doi:10.7448/IAS.18.1.19462. "Eugenics." *Merriam-Webster*, Merriam-Webster,www.merriam-webster.com/dictionary/eugenics.

Hasegawa, Kyoko. "Lifetimes of Pain: Victims of Japan's Forced Sterilization Program Hope for Justice, or at Least an Apology." *The Japan Times*, 20 Apr. 2018, www.japantimes.jp/news/2018/04/20/national/social-issues/lifetimes-pain-victims-japans-forced-sterilizati on-program-hope-justice-least-apology/#.XJFlvyhKg2w.

Kovarik, Jacquelyn. "Why Don't We Talk About Peru's Forced Sterilizations?" *The New Republic*, 8 Oct. 2018, newrepublic.com/article/151599/dont-talk-perus-forced-sterilizations.

"Nicaragua." *UNAIDS*, 11 Nov. 2007, www.unaids.org/en/regionscountries/countries/nicaragua.

Olivera, Roxana. "Against Their Will." *New Internationalist*, no. 493, June 2016, pp. 30–32. *EBSCOhost*, search.ebscohost.com/login.aspx?direct=true&db=asn&AN=115245332&site=e host-live&scope=site.

Patel, P. (2017). Forced sterilization of women as discrimination. *Public Health Reviews, 38* doi:http://dx.doi.org/10.1186/s40985-017-0060-9

Rivard, Lauren. "America's Hidden History: The Eugenics Movement." *Nature News*, Nature Publishing Group, 18 Sept. 2014, www.nature.com/scitable/forums/genetics-generation/america-s-hidden-history-the-eugenics-movement-123919444.

Szilvasi, Marek. "Intersectional Discrimination of Romani Women Forcibly Sterilized in the Former Czechoslovakia and Czech Republic." *Health and Human Rights*, Harvard University Press, Dec. 2017, www.ncbi.nlm.nih.gov/pmc/articles/PMC5739354/.

# THE DEMAND FOR CHANGE

## Cambria Tiemann

Cambria Tiemann, a marketing major from Linden, Michigan, says "I often think back to the strategies that Professor Craig Hulst taught me, like finding reliable information for my research, and I've applied them to other classes." She encourages current first-year writing students to use the Writing Center; she says, "I went to the Writing Center multiple times throughout the semester and the consultants helped me a ton."

Crowds of people scrambling to avoid bullets, tear gas and water cannons headed their way, flames sprawled across the roads, smoke blocking the view of what's ahead, and yelling coming from people in all directions. No, this isn't a scene from a dystopian novel, this is what Iraq faced head-on. In October 1, 2019, the Prime Minister of Iraq, Adil Abdul-Mahdi, authoritatively mandated an internet blockage and a nationwide curfew in response to protests conducted by the youth of Iraq (Cornish). All movements of people and vehicles had been restricted in an attempt to put an end to the riots taking place in Baghdad and in surrounding cities (Cornish). Furthermore, with rising frustrations amongst young Iraq citizens and aggressive reactions against the protesters, Baghdad and Iraq were clearly in a state of peril.

Divisions between the young citizens of Iraq and the government are nothing new; however, recently, tensions have escalated greatly between the two. For years, the impoverished youth have been subject to backlash from their own government. With 25% of Iraq's youth unable to find jobs and accusations of government corruption, it has become evident that these adolescents are ready to demand a change from their government ("Iraq Protests"). Gattee Zowayer, an Iraq protester, when discussing what the protesters wanted, stated, "We want jobs, lands for the poor people and for the people who are corrupt to be made accountable" (Rubin "All"). Zowayer, along with the rest of the protesters, are upset about the government corruption taking place. Iraq's government is constitutionally defined as an Islamic, democratic, federal parliamentary republic ("Government of Iraq"). In the Iraq government, Abdul-Mahdi, holds the majority of the executive power and although he has only been in power since October, 2018, he is already under intense scrutiny for not providing jobs and income for the youth of his country (Cornish). The citizens are undeniably blaming Abdul-Mahdi for the majority of the country's shortcomings.

It is, however, a bit more complicated than simply assigning blame to the current ruler. According to John Davison, "after decades of war against its neighbors... the defeat of the Islamic State insurgency in 2017 means Iraq is now at peace and free to trade for the first extended period since the 1970s. Oil output is at record levels" (Davison). This means that Iraq has become a single resource (oil) export-dependent country. With oil as their primary source of income, this invaluable resource affects the country's overall distribution of wealth. While statistically many countries with a single export resource tend to struggle with political corruption, "the situation is much worse in Iraq because corruption has become embedded in the structure of all the main political parties" (Dyer). The main political parties are in charge of one or more government ministries and instead of utilizing their power to help provide for all members of the country, they often fixate on creating jobs and distributing wealth to only those within their own party (Dyer). This, in turn, "allowed certain individuals and groups to enrich themselves and expand their influence [while the rest of the] country's population continued to endure severe economic hardship and poor public services" (Najjar). The corrupt political system has become a substantial issue with the youth population who are unaffiliated with a political party as there are no jobs left for them. These young Iraq civilians have become increasingly frustrated with the state of their nation and are seeking out drastic changes.

The demand for change presented itself in the form of protests beginning on October 1, 2019 in Baghdad, the capital of Iraq, and other cities throughout the country. The protests were small at first but after multiple social media postings, the protests progressed at an increasingly steady rate. The majority of these young postgraduate protesters are students who are fed up with government corruption and are demanding jobs and better infrastructure (Davison). Along with this, protesters are demanding for the abolishment of the sectarianism type government and instead a new form of government that represents them (Bunyan). These protests instill a sense of fear in the government due to their increasing growth rate and lack of leader/political affiliation. Without a main source to these protests, the government has had a difficult time controlling them. When the protests grew and anger amongst civilians began to build at an alarming rate, the government was forced to take action. On October 3, 2019, Abdul-Mahdi declared a city-wide curfew throughout Baghdad. This curfew strictly limited the movement of almost all individuals and vehicles (Chulov). Along with a curfew, Abdul-Mahdi also implemented an Internet blockage which restricted access to social media sites and internet access ("Iraq Protests"). According to Netblocks, "the state imposed a near-total telecommunication shutdown in most regions, severely limiting press coverage and transparency around the ongoing crisis". This blockage was used in an effort to prevent protesters from congregating and forming bigger revolts. This was also a government attempt to keep Iraq's current situation concealed from the rest of the world. Nonetheless, these protest regulation attempts failed miserably as the revolts gained in power and in numbers.

As the protests expanded, the force of the government's security used against their civilians increased as well (see fig. 1). Security forces were said to have fired live ammunition, tear gas, rubber bullets and water cannons to clear the crowds ("Seven Dead").

As of December 2, 2019, throughout these periods of protest, "at least 420 people have reportedly been killed and 17,000 injured" ("The Iraq Protests Explained"). Not only are the security forces a threat to civilians during protests, but the fear of these guards follows activists everywhere they go. The Human Rights Watch, interviewed and talked to many of these protesters and their families to get a better idea of just how intense the situation in Iraq was. One activist they spoke to, Maher Hassan Satar, said that pictures were taken of him from the earlier protests and within a couple days a SWAT officer that had seen his picture online dragged him behind a vehicle and beat him with a plastic pipe ("Iraq: Government"). "The brother of another protester claims that his brother has not been heard from since he went to a Baghdad protest on October 3, 2019 . . . He said he went to the police and security offices but has found no sign of him." ("Iraq: Government"). The death, disappearance and violence against protesters by the security force members is getting out of hand and a withdrawal of armed forces and a response from the government is in order.

Fig. 1: Iraqi protesters run from tear gas fired by security forces at Baghdad's Khallani square during ongoing anti-government demonstrations on Nov. 12 (Mansour et al).

In response to the out of hand attacks performed by armed forces, the government has made a slight attempt to control the situation. A report made by the New York Times discussed the government action taken to punish armed forces. The report stated that, "[at] least four senior military officers whose operations were in Baghdad were among those referred for prosecution. In addition, the police commanders of at least six provinces south of Baghdad where protesters were shot ... lost their jobs" (Rubin "Iraq"). Another source stated that, "Prime Minister Adil Abdul-Mahdi signed off on the recommendations of an investigative panel on October 22. The panel recommended firing senior security officials and investigating senior officials" ("Iraq: Government"). The firing and prosecution of officers is certainly a step in the right direction; however, more needs to be done. While, it is somewhat reassuring that the Iraq regime is taking some steps toward resolving this quandary, they still have a long way to go toward ensuring the safety and well-being of their citizens.

Following Abdul-Mahdi and the governments insufficient attempts at fixing the problem, the protests still continued. The growing severity of these protests instilled pressure on the prime minister. With increased backlash and demand from the Iraq civilians, Abdul-Mahdi decided to resign (Ibrahim). In the article "Iraq's Striking Students Defiant amid Unrelenting Protests.", Hussein, an activist who is currently attending medical school was asked his thoughts on this resignation. Hussein responded, "Abdul Mahdi's resignation means nothing. We're continuing our strike until the electoral law changes. Unless that happens, our main ask for a complete overhaul of the political system can't be achieved." Even with the prime minister out of power, the citizens of Iraq will not stop protesting until an effective change is made.

In the aftermath of the event, the actions taken by the government and resignation of the prime minister were not nearly enough to correct the problems engulfing the nation of Iraq. If proper action is not taken in the face of this tragedy, the tensions could continue to heighten. The future of the country could be dire if major adjustments are not made. Currently, the situation in Iraq is looking eerily similar to another struggling country who had impatient citizens. Back in the 1990's, a similar trend amongst the youth in Afghanistan was taking place. During this time, the Islamic extremist group, referred to as the Taliban, came to power. This group was composed of mainly youth with too much free time. A common trend no matter where in the world involves adolescents who are often found searching for a purposeful outlet to fulfill their lives. "When the government and society in general fail to channel this energy into positive actions, young people look for other sources of purpose" (Ahmadi). This tendency to search for a source of purpose was found amongst the youth of Afghanistan who in turn decided to join the Taliban. Unfortunately, these other sources are not always in the civilians or their countries best interest.

The Taliban left an astounding impact on their country that was nothing short of devastating. Their extremist reign starting in 1996 and ending around 2001, quickly became detrimental to the country of Afghanistan. In a four-year tie span, the Taliban committed fifteen different massacres of civilians (Gargan). An article by Gargan "describes victims being lined up, their hands tied behind their backs, shot and dumped in mass graves... [and]

civilians being beaten to death". Along with the annihilation of innocent Afghanistan inhabitants, "by 1999, the Taliban forced hundreds of thousands of people from the region and destroyed their farms, shops and homes" (Schneider). The Taliban also carried out a cultural genocide. Temples of the Hindu and Sikh were destroyed along with statues of Buddha. These were deemed to be "unislamic" by the extreme Taliban members (Kinloch and Mohan 224). The members of the Taliban were able to expeditiously disband and tear apart their country leaving behind a tremendous amount of death and destruction.

If Iraq isn't careful they could start to see a similar fate. According to Belquis Ahmadi, "in Afghanistan, the typical explanation for violent extremism is that it arises in response to large-scale poverty and endemic high unemployment." The severe level of poverty and youth unemployment is comparable to the situation taking place in Iraq. With the youth of Iraq in a state of financial hardships and at a loss for jobs (similar to those in Afghanistan back in the 1990's/early 2000s) they have already started to join forces to revolt against this corruption. If the Iraq government is not careful the youth of their country could follow in the same footsteps as the Taliban. In essence, the government needs to take action in order to prevent this from happening.

The government still has a long way to go if they want to stop these protests and improve the standard of living in their country. As Amnesty International's Middle East and North Africa Director Heba Morayef said, "the government of Iraq has a duty to protect its people's right to life, as well as to gather and express their views. This bloodbath must stop now, and those responsible for it must be brought to justice" ("Iraq Authorities"). The government must hold those accountable for the death of the protesters. Hopefully, this will help to prevent future attacks. However, just the prosecution of the armed forces won't be enough if Iraq wants to see change. Iraq's government also needs to restructure their political party system to ensure that the main political parties are not in control of the distribution of wealth. This will allow for jobs to be created for the youth and for an overall better quality of life for the civilians. If the government does not take action and act quickly, the country could fall back into another civil war, or worse, the protesters could form a power-hungry group similar to that of the Taliban.

Fig. 2: Protester stands by the "Wall of Wishes" (Reuters).

While the protests have unfortunately brought about killings and devastation in Iraq, they have also brought as sense of hope and unity amongst the citizens. "Just off Baghdad's Tahrir Square, ground zero for a protest movement that remains unbowed despite the deaths of hundreds of demonstrators in a government crackdown, protesters have set up a "wall of wishes" (see fig. 2) (Graff).

This "wall of wishes" features thousands of post-it notes stuck on the wall of an abandoned public bathroom. The post-it notes written by activists have wishes, prayers or comments about the future of Iraq on them (Graff). A report by Reuters was done where they asked several of the activists partaking in the wall of wished what they wrote on their sticky note. One young woman, Fatima Awad, wrote "'I used to hate Iraq before October 25, now I'm proud of it'" (Graff). October 25 was the first day that activists attempted to raid the Green Zone of government buildings (Graff). Awad also commented in an interview with Reuter that "Before, we did not have a future, and no one would protest because everyone was scared. Now, we're all gathered at Tahrir Square,". Those who started the wall now wish to compile all of the notes into a book (Graff). The citizens of Iraq are targeting their frustrations into unity and togetherness. This unification is a symbol of hope and is a step in the right direction for the future of Iraq.

The Iraq protests that started in October of 2019 have instilled fear in the government, prompting a nationwide curfew, internet blockage and the killing of harmless protesters. The youth protesters demanded change and came together with great strength in order to fight for the enrichment of the country. In order for this to happen, the government must ensure that the sectarianist political system is overthrown. This will require an enormous amount of changes to their policies, political systems and wealth distribution. It may appear as quite challenging but it is what needs to happen in order to stop Iraq from being portrayed as that dystopian novel. To avoid this it will take strong leadership, the overwhelming support of the people willing to stand up against the current regime, and most importantly, time.

*Word Count: 2523*

## Works Cited

Ahmadi, Belquis. "Afghan Youth and Extremists." *United States Institute of Peace*, 29 Dec. 2016, https://www.usip.org/publications/2015/08/afghan-youth-and-extremists.

Bunyan, Rachael. "Iraq Protests: What Do the Protesters Want?" *Time*, 13 Nov. 2019, https://time.com/5723831/iraq-protests/.

Chulov, Martin. "Internet Blackout in Iraq as Death Toll from Violent Protests Rises." *The Guardian*, Guardian News and Media, 3 Oct. 2019, https://www.theguardian.com/world/2019/oct/03/internet-down-across-iraq-third-day-protests.

Cornish, Chloe. "Iraq Announces Curfew in Baghdad as Protests Escalate." *Financial Times*, Financial Times, 3 Oct. 2019, https://www.ft.com/content/6922ff3a-e5b9-11e9-b112-9624ec9edc59.

Davison, John. "Explainer: Deadly Civil Unrest—What Is Happening in Iraq?" *Reuters*, Thomson Reuters, 3 Oct. 2019, https://www.reuters.com/article/us-iraq-protests-explain/explainer-deadly-civil-unrest-what-is-happening-in-iraq idUSKBN1WI 10E.

Dyer, Gwynne. "Hopelessness among the Young in Iraq." *Cyprus Mail*, 8 Oct. 2019, https://cyprus-mail.com/2019/10/08/hopelessness-among-the-young-in-iraq/.

Gargan, Edward. "Confidential UN Report Details Mass Killings of Civilian Villagers." *MASSACRES OF CIVILIAN VILLAGERS AT LEAST 15 TIMES BY TALIBAN*, Newsday, 12 Oct. 2001, https://web.archive.org/web/20021 118162327/http://www.papillonsartpalace.com/massacre.htm.

"Government of Iraq." *GraphicMaps*, 17 Jan. 2018, https://www.graphicmaps.com/iraq/government.

Graff, Peter. "'When Will the Bloodshed Stop?' - Notes and Prayers on Iraq's Wall of Wishes." Edited by Mark Heinrich, *Reuters*, 26 Nov. 2019, https://www.reuters.com/article/us-iraq-protests-wall/when-will-the-bloodshed-stop-notes-and-prayers-on-iraqs-wall-of-wishes-idUSKBN1Y0253.

Ibrahim, Arwa. "Iraq's Striking Students Defiant amid Unrelenting Protests." *News | Al Jazeera*, 2 Dec. 2019, https://www.aljazeera.com/news/2019/11/iraq-striking-students-defiant-unrelenting-protests-191130140035735.html.

"Iraq: Government Promises Action On Security Force Abuse." *Human Rights Watch*, 27 Oct. 2019, https://www.hrw.org/news/2019/10/24/iraq-government-promises-action-security-force-abuse

"Iraqi Authorities Must Rein in Security Forces to Prevent a Bloodbath, after Six More Protesters Killed in Baghdad." *Iraq: Rein in Security Forces to Prevent a Bloodbath | Amnesty International*, https://www.amnesty.org/en/latest/news/2019/11/iraq-rein-in-security-forces-to-prevent-a-bloodbath/. Accessed 05 Oct. 2019.

"Iraq Protests: All the Latest Updates." *News | Al Jazeera*, 9 Oct. 2019, https://www.aljazeera.com/news/2019/10/iraq-protests-latest-updates-191004085506824.html.

"The Iraq Protests Explained in 100 and 500 Words." *BBC News*, 2 Dec. 2019, https://www.bbc.com/news/world-middle-east-50595212.

Kinloch, Charles, and Raj P. Mohan. *Genocide: Approaches, Case Studies, And Responses*. Algora Publishing, December 1, 2005.

Mansour, Renad et al. "These Iraqi Militias are Attacking Protesters and Getting Away with it. Here's Why." *The Washington Post*, November 18, 2019, https://www.washingtonpost.com/politics/2019/11/18/these-iraqi-militias-are-attacking-protesters-getting-away-with-it-heres-why/.

Najjar, Farah. "Iraq Protesters Insist on System Overhaul after US Call for Vote." *News | Al Jazeera*, 11 Nov. 2019, https://www.aljazeera.com/news/2019/11/iraq-protesters-insist-system-overhaul-call-vote-191111105449265.html.

Reuters. "Baghdad's Wall of Wishes is Source of Hope." *Y Net News*. November 27, 2019. https://www.ynetnews.com/article/r1GHVxihB.

Rubin, Alissa J. "'All of Them Are Thieves': Iraqis Defy Security Forces to Protest Corruption." *The New York Times*, 25 Oct. 2019, https://www.nytimes.com/2019/10/25/world/middleeast/iraq-protests.html.

---. "Iraq Will Prosecute Military and Police Leaders Over Protest Shootings." *The New York Times*, 22 Oct. 2019, https://www.nytimes.com/ 2019/10/22/world/middleeast/iraq-protests-generals-court.html.

Schneider, A. "Re-Creating Afghanistan: Returning to Istalif." *Re-Creating Afghanistan: Returning to Istalif*, NPR, 8 Jan. 2002, https://web.archive.org/web/20131023072254 / http://www.npr.org/programs/morning/features/2002/aug/afghanistan/.

"Seven Dead, Hundreds Injured in Iraq as Anti-Government Protests Escalate." *ABC News*, 3 Oct. 2019, https://www.abc.net.au/news/2019-10-03/iraq-declares-curfews-as-gunfights-rage-and-protests-spread-nat/11570632.

# PROFESSIONAL WRESTLING IS ART

### Caleb Wolfe

For Caleb Wolfe, a Writing major from Dowagiac, Michigan, Professor Susan Laidlaw-McCreery's first-year writing class gave him a chance to explore his creativity. He explains that his class "essentially unraveled everything I learned about writing in high school and instilled in me a sense of freedom and liberty as a writer." Caleb also "found seeking feedback to be the most crucial aspect of [his] success in the class... Asking for an opinion may seem like a vulnerable thing to do, but it will only help you in the long run."

"RIP HIS HEAD OFF!" My dad's strained voice screams with burning passion loud enough to draw the entire arena's attention over to us. Embarrassed, I slump down in my seat, trying to focus on the match in front of me. "I'm not with him!" I shyly mouth to the people sitting next to me. His yelling persists throughout the rest of the show, but as the night goes on, I begin to understand his genuine excitement. I mean, for goodness sake, I'm sitting in the middle of a sold out Van Andel Arena watching the one and only John Cena lay the smackdown on his poor opponent in the ring. *How could anyone not love this?!*

"You know it's *fake*, right?" A simple snide remark that stings the most dedicated fans of professional wrestling. There is a massive stigma surrounding the entire concept of televised wrestling promotions around the world. Many people write it off as a joke, refusing to buy into what has become a multi-million dollar industry in America alone. Some even claim that it is a silly performance masquerading as a sport. Well, the unsurprising truth behind professional wrestling is that it is scripted, rather than simply fake. In fact, Vince McMahon, chairman of perhaps the largest and most globally recognizable wrestling promotion, World Wrestling Entertainment (WWE), publicly admitted in February of 1989 that professional wrestling should be defined as, "An activity in which participants struggle hand-in-hand primarily for the purpose of providing entertainment to spectators rather than conducting a bona fide athletic contest" (Hoy-Browne). Thus coining the term "sports entertainment." Following the aftermath of

McMahon's truth, the industry actually grew in popularity, despite the mysterious aura that had shrouded the minds of impressionable audiences for years being lifted.

Consider wrestling then as a form of art. I know one might be wondering, "How could two grown men throwing each other around violently in colorful tights possibly be art?!" In a way, it is very much like theatre, in which actors assume roles, scenes and settings are created to propel a story, and the audience watches respectively. The people attending those productions are aware that what they are seeing is fictional, yet they suspend their disbelief for the duration of the shows in order to fully indulge themselves in the worlds in which they occur (Workman). In the realm of wrestling exists such drama. Kayfabe, the convention of presenting staged performances as genuine or authentic, rests in both the minds of the fans who choose to experience wrestling, and the wrestlers themselves. The term, most closely associated with wrestling, was coined in the late 20th century, with many speculation as to the clear origin of it. Some reasonably believe that it was used as a carnival slang for the phrase "be fake" when referring to the then rising spectacle of choreographed combat ("Kayfabe"). Kayfabe encourages men and women employed under any given promotion to completely become their character portrayed in the ring and on television, just like an actor in a play enables themself to fully assume their role. In doing so, ordinary people like Terry Bollea could become mega heroes with names like Hulk Hogan. One woman interviewed at a show expressed her love for professional wrestlers, declaring, "These people are artists as well. They have to be creative. Wrestling is choreographed art" (Deeter-Schmelz and Sojka). Night after night, these charismatic and brave athletes put on thrilling spectacles, sacrificing the very safety of their bodies for the sake of entertaining millions.

*WHACK!* The sound of steel meeting flesh as one wrestler swings a chair over another's head resonates throughout a packed arena. Although trained to deliver such acts safely, there is no denying that professional wrestlers experience *real* pain. All the death-defying moves fans are accustomed to seeing, like piledrivers and chair shots, take hours upon hours of rigorous practice and preparation to pull of properly to reduce the most amount of injuries on the in-ring participants. In 1993, Sharon Mazer of the University Press of Mississippi spent time in a training gym observing wrestlers hard at work. She noted, "Professional wrestlers learn the rules of the game as athletic skills, as performance practice, and as masculine ethos. Through a kinetic process of observation, repetition, demonstration, and correction in interaction with other wrestlers, they imprint the moves in their bodies." One wrong move or mistimed step could severely incapacitate these very mortal beings. According to spine surgeon and sports injury medical analyst Michael A. Gleiber, wrestlers are at high risk for concussions and back related injuries due to the repetitive motions and impact they endure frequently. Repeated trauma to the head can lead directly to the brain disease Chronic Traumatic Encephalopathy, which coincides with symptoms of depression, increased aggression, and even dementia. In light of everything that could go wrong during any given wrestling match, referees officiating them must be able to immediately notice any sign of legitimate harm to the performers. Even with all the dangerous risks looming over them, wrestlers go on with the show.

Of course, there has to be a certain appeal to the product of wrestling. Most wrestling fans know what it's like to be pestered by friends who can't comprehend why anyone would actually watch it. Conveniently enough, several studies and interviews have been conducted to discover motives and consequential reactions for tuning in week after week to engage in viewership. Using laddering research to collect numerous, often subconscious, answers from attendants at WWE events, Doctor Dawn R. Deeter-Schmelz and Doctor Jane Z. Sojka, professors of Marketing at Ohio University, identified key elements that draw dedicated fans back time and time again. The majority of participants interviewed described feeling a sense of belonging through watching wrestling with groups of friends. It could be concluded that a special bond is created from joining together to partake in WWE's product, giving people something to look forward to and a reason to see each other. Discussing current wrestling trends, possible storyline outcomes, and favorite match moments leads to continual communication and commonality for those involved. It's almost like professional wrestling is a soap opera for men (though women do enjoy it as well), and just like middle aged women get together to watch *Days of Our Lives* over a glass of white wine, guys get together to watch other guys dive off ladders and through tables over a couple of brewskies. Same thing, really.

Similarly to genuine sports, fans of professional wrestling typically align themselves with particular superstars, just like fans of football, for instance, identify with their favorite teams. Audience participation is crucial in live wrestling events, and it is not uncommon for a crowd to cheer for faces, or the "good guys," and boo the heels, or the "bad guys." Sam Ford, research affiliate with the Massachusetts Institute of Technology's Program in Comparative Media, provides a fascinating insight into the aspect of fan involvement. Using a series of interviews and personal examination, he explains how a fair amount of audience members assume an acting role themselves at live events, receiving immense enjoyment from their engaged experiences. Chanting performers' names, cheering for a hero's victory, or even heckling the villains, generates audience heat that Ford explains drives fans to get carried away in the moment, even though they know they are watching a scripted storyline. Psychologically, spectators are drawn into this drama for many reasons. The action happening in the ring taps deep into their minds, triggering and subsequently fulfilling their own fantasies. This sensation can also be described as living vicariously through the performers (Deeter-Schmelz and Sojka). When a fan favorite wrestler wins a match, those who supported them feel a sense of pride, giving great testimonial for the wrestler's character and craft. In a way, that same pride is multiplied in a lot of fans, because they feel that by cheering for their favorite star, they helped them win. Indeed, there is tremendous appreciation for professional wrestling. Audience engagement and overall storyline performance on the wrestlers' behalf go hand in hand, creating a truly special spectacle when connected seamlessly.

A pained groan escapes the lips of the wrestler on the receiving end of John Cena's signature Five Knuckle Shuffle move, which is basically just a faceful of fist that never fails to rile up the audience. We all know what's coming next. Piecing together a beautiful sequence, John Cena heaves his muscular foe up over his shoulders and promptly slams him down on the mat. Hooking his leg, he goes for the pin, sending the much smaller referee sprawling down to make the count. My father is now redder than a cherry in the face, completely possessed by aggressive glee. The piercing ring bell chimes erratically over his boisterous cheering, bringing resolution to what has been an electric night of wrestling. *1! 2! 3!* This paper is over!

*Word Count: 1478*

Works Cited

Deeter-Schmelz, Dawn R., and Jane Z. Sojka. "Wrestling with American Values: An Exploratory Investigation of World Wrestling Entertainment as a product-based Subculture." *Journal of Consumer Behaviour*, vol. 4, no. 2, 2004, pp. 132–143.

Gleiber, Michael A. "The Unscripted Side of Professional Wrestling." *The Huffington Post*, TheHuffingtonPost.com, 10 June 2015, www.huffingtonpost.com/michael-a-gleiber-md/the-unscripted-side-of-pr_b_7040344.html.

Hoy-Browne, Richard. "Historic Moments in Wrestling Part 6: Vince McMahon Admits Wrestling." *The Independent*, Independent Digital News and Media, 30 May 2014, www.independent.co.uk/sport/general/wwe-mma-wrestling/historic-moments-in-wrestlin g-part-6-vince-mcmahon-admits-wrestling-is-predetermined-9461429.html.

"Kayfabe: It's Illusive and Elusive." *Merriam-Webster*, Merriam-Webster, www.merriam-webster.com/words-at-play/word-origin-kayfabe.

Mazer, Sharon. *Professional Wrestling: Sport and Spectacle.* U niversity Press of Mississippi, Jackson, 1998.

Workman, Mark E. "Dramaturgical Aspects of Professional Wrestling Matches." *Folklore Forum*, vol. 10, 1977, pp. 14–20.

# MINIMALISM IN OUR DIGITAL WORLD

### Kaya Dahlquist

Kaya Dahlquist, who comes from Cadillac, Michigan, is a Hospitality and Tourism Management Major with a minor in Advertising and Public Relations. As a student in Professor Jason Lenz's class, Kaya found her greatest area of growth was in making the "change from a high school writing voice to a college writing voice," which she accomplished by working hard at incorporating feedback from her professor.

With Netflix shows, bloggers, vloggers, and countless articles being posted, the minimalist lifestyle has taught thousands of people, including myself, that having less in their life means more. The day I decided to become a minimalist I entered a world where I learned that my material possessions don't guarantee my happiness and living by intention is more fulfilling than any of my full junk drawers. However, when Apple released the feature on the iPhone that allowed its users to see how much time they truly spent on their devices I entered a whole new area of clutter in my life that I thought I had rid myself of when I dropped off my numerous donate boxes at Goodwill. I picked up my phone and received a very shocking truth about my digital habits. On the average day I pick my phone up 82 times, get 499 notifications, and spend 3 hours and 18 minutes scrolling through several of my social media platforms, making my total usage for the week 23 hours and 10 minutes of screen time, showing me I waste almost one entire day sitting and scrolling through my phone.

Like most of the population, I thought a minimalist lifestyle was just about decluttering your life by getting rid of your material things and. However, after realizing my screen time habits I decided that I needed to do some serious research. After some time of researching, I found that minimalism is, "a lifestyle that helps people question what things add value to their lives. By clearing the clutter from life's path, we can all make room for the most important aspects of life: health, relationships, passion, growth, and contribution." and that it is just as much of a mental mindset and intentions as it is with our physical objects (Wignall). However, within the minimalist lifestyle a new aspect called digital minimalism has emerged within the evolving times of our current digital age. The concept of digital minimalism has started emerging as we spend more time looking at our screens and developing more of a relationship with our devices than people around us. Digital minimalism isn't completely getting rid of technology in our everyday lives but is instead describes the both physical and mental parts of minimalism and makes people question if their technology usage adds any value or intention to their life. Without addressing digital minimalism problem areas and following the three principles of digital minimalism no one can reach the true meaning of the minimalist lifestyle.

Digital minimalism is defined by Cal Newport as, "a philosophy that helps you question what digital communication tools (and behaviors surrounding these tools) add the most value to your life" which mirrors the traditional look on minimalism where people look at their physical objects (Newport). However, digital minimalism problem areas are best described split into two parts; the physical clutter that it can cause in our lives and the clutter that it causes in our mental health and emotional lives. The physical clutter that is solved by digital minimalism can be best related to the traditional minimalism that people see represented in the media. The physical aspect of digital minimalism includes the decluttering of old technologies that we hold onto, and digital files that pile up in our devices. As times change and our technology evolves into the next newest edition, we often hold onto our old gadgets because they hold some sentimental value, but the new addition offers, "cognitively rewarding bells and whistles" that eventually just becomes "addictive for the mirage of social engagement" (*800 CEO Read: Digital Minimalism: Choosing a Focused Life in a Noisy World*). However, as we hold onto our old gadgets we keep a cycle going as the new technology becomes the old technology that is then kept in our sentimental junk drawer with the later version of the same device. According to digital minimalism, if the technology isn't useful or beneficial to any parts of our lives there is no need to keep it. But, there is also physical technological clutter that we can't hold in our hands. According to minimalist consultant Cary Fortin people usually "shift from physical clutter to digital clutter" because we can't see it ("The Minimalism Movement"). This refers to all of the downloads, files, pictures, and unneeded things that we save onto our digital devices that take up needed space in our hard drives. People nowadays do almost everything digitally by downloading everything that used to be a physical copy we could hold in our hands now onto our laptops. With the thousands of files, we download, one or two times, they continue to build up creating an endless list of unknown files on our computer that serve no use to us other than taking up space in our digital footprint. Just like having physical clutter is stressful for most people, having digital clutter is stressful as well. Liz Duck-Chong describes the release of unneeded digital baggage as "like a cleaving, a blade cutting clean through tender flesh" and that after everything was gone she can now "make more room in my head for moments that feel significant, and the moments I do share with people are more valuable in turn" (Duck-Chong). With the dismissal of old technologies and unneeded digital clutter we can free up our space and our minds.

With the buildup of unneeded data, we lose what is useful and beneficial not only within our devices but also within our emotional and mental health. With emails coming in, social media begging for likes, and snapchat streaks to uphold it's easy for the average human to become lost in digital clutter that instead of building up in our living rooms, builds up in our minds. We consistently put our intentions for our digital life first and our intentions for our physical life and mental health second. The Center for Humane Technology projects their mission statement "Technology is hijacking our minds and society" and helps develop the case that the "zero-sum race four our finite attention" that each app is fighting for drastically builds the amount of quality time we spend on our screens (Center for Humane Technology). In turn, this starts to take our attention away from the most important parts of our lives and our intentions. A study conducted by the Department of Computer Information Systems at Middle Tennessee State University (MTSU) established that a person's social media usage causes problems in with "attention control" and "multitasking", along with causing problems in people's "well-being model" ("Does"). After analyzing "the effects of personal social media usage on task performance" and " the effects that personal media usage has on individuals' technostress and happiness levels", MTSU found that "social media usage was found to negatively affect performance" while people "claim that they are multitasking" and "social media usage is positively associated with technostress" that increases in "people who use great amounts of technology" everyday ("Does"). As a population we have enough chaos in our everyday lives to sort through, however, when we add an entire new world of apps and online profiles to the mix it's even harder to focus on our mental state and our concentration. As our minds start to be clouded by the amount of time we spend on our devices, our mental state can start to dwindle as well. The more information we take in through our screens the more overwhelmed and less-focused we can feel. With the short-term escape and isolation that technology offers us we think of it as a place of safety, however, it causes more damage than we notice. Nick Wignall describes the short emotional relief causing problems by leading "to more consistent suffering in the long term" because it "makes it much more difficult to confront them when we must" (Wignall). If we always are trying to escape our problems every time they arise we ignore the problem and the intentions behind the problem. Wignall also describes the isolation that our minds go into when we consistently escape into our digital world saying that it causes "disconnect from other people in our lives" and even our own reality (Wignall). This only leads to more stress and anxiety when we are forced to interact socially and solve problems in real time. Our minds can be trained to self-destruct at any moment and they can be trained to endure through problems. However, if you spend all the time using your intentions on your smartphone, you're less likely to endure through anything.

After finding what area the digital clutter comes from most people have the same question; "What do I do now to stop my digital clutter?". Nick Wignall set up a study to answer this very question by using what he deems are the "3 Basic Principles of Digital Minimalism" and outlines way that people can start their digital minimalism journey (Wignall). The first principle that Wignall lists is "Technology use should be intentional not habitual" and shows how to combat the addictive nature of our technology that leads to us mindlessly overusing our devices that interferes with our everyday values and intentions (Wignall). The second principle is "Technology is for making stuff not feeling better" that tells how to combat using our devices for short term emotional relief for easy escape from our confrontations (Wignall). Finally, the third and what Wignall deems the "most important principle" lists "Technology should never come before people" that tells how to combat the social isolation that social media causes (Wignall).

To start living by these intentions Wignall offers a process to follow that offers a easier transition into the world of digital minimalism. This process starts with the person choosing a period of time where they go mostly tech free or completely tech free and delete all unneeded apps, podcasts, subscriptions, and turn off all their notifications on their devices in order to make sure the person only logs into a platform when they have a specific need to. After detaching from the digital clutter the person should then go back to the basics as far as their digital habits including buying a newspaper instead of reading it off your phone, listening to the radio instead of podcasts or YouTube, reading paper copy books rather than on your phone, and watch limited amounts of TV rather than binging on a streaming platform. Finally, the person should severely limit the amount that they text and personal email people, but instead make time to call people and talk to them instead.

Digital minimalism isn't completely giving up every use of technology and all its benefits, it's about being intentional and using technology to our needs and using it intentionally. This concept was harder for me to start to adapt to than it was to part with almost all my belongings. I found that I was truly addicted to my technology and all the digital clutter that came with it. Deleting my social media apps, podcasts, and limiting my messaging sounded like someone was threatening to cut of a couple of my fingers and I felt the automatic weight of anxiety sit into my chest that usually happens whenever I misplace my phone for more than a minute. However, it was those exact feelings that showed me that I needed to take a lot closer of a look at my daily routine and intentions that I chose to live by. I needed to remind myself that minimalism is more than donating my things and cute Instagram pictures. It is a way of life that offers a clean headspace and clear intentions for life, which in my case was clearly being blocked by my screen time. So, after a purge of my electronic platforms and the turning off of all my notifications I started out on a new journey that will hopefully go below the surface of a new blog post.

*Word Count: 2003*

Work Cited

*Center for Humane Technology*, humanetech.com/problem#the-
     way-forward.
"Does Personal Social Media Usage Affect Efficiency and Well-
     Being?" *Computers in Human Behavior*, Pergamon, 21
     Jan. 2015, www.sciencedirect.com/science/article/pii/
     S0747563215000096#!
Duck-Chong, Liz. "Digital Minimalism: How do You KonMari
     a 10-Year Text Message History?"*ProQuest*, Feb 26,
     2019, http://search.proquest.com.ezproxy.gvsu.edu/
     docview/2185978223?accountid=39473.
"The Minimalism Movement: Where Does Your Tech Fit
     In?" *Forbes,* 27 June 2018, www.forbes.com/sites/
     capitalone/2017/11/28/the-minimalism-movement-where-
     does-your-tech-fit-in/#60f0d52a784a.
Newport , Cal. "On Digital Minimalism ." *Cal Newport*, 18
     Dec. 2016, calnewport.com/blog/2016/12/18/on-digital-
     minimalism/.
Wignall, Nick. "What Is Digital Minimalism?" *Nick Wignall*,
     6 Feb. 2019, nickwignall.com/what-is-digital-minimalism/.
*800 CEO Read: Digital Minimalism: Choosing a Focused
     Life in a Noisy World.* Newstex, Chatham, 2019.
     *ProQuest*, http://search.proquest.com.ezproxy.gvsu.edu/
     docview/2177277016?accountid=39473.

# ZERO WASTE

### Briana Dara

As a student in Professor Teresa Gibbons' class, Briana Dara, a Criminal Justice major from Grand Haven, Michigan, used her own curiosity to inspire her research on zero waste. She explains, "I always wondered where things like damaged goods went, and with my own exploration, I found out more about it through writing this essay." She encourages current students to "find things you are very passionate about; it makes it much easier to write these essays."

Browsing through the aisles of my favorite grocery store, I found the bamboo toothbrush I was looking for. I have been buying bamboo toothbrushes for two years because I try my best to live a zero-waste lifestyle. They last for about two months, and everything from the bristles to the handle are biodegradable. Because of this, they do not end up in landfills for long. When I brought home the toothbrush, I tossed out the packaging and then I thought about it: the biodegradable toothbrushes I have been purchasing come in carboard and plastic packaging. The cardboard is biodegradable, but the plastic is not. This company that manufactures a zero-waste product was ironically creating garbage. How many companies promote zero-waste but do not live up to their claims? What are they doing to contribute towards this movement? Although it is nearly impossible to be a completely zero-waste company, innovative solutions can create less waste for the environment.

Living a zero-waste lifestyle is not only environmentally friendly, but it makes me feel ethically responsible for the planet. It is important to know where our trash is going and although we recycle, most of our trash ends up elsewhere. "While 84% of the solid wastes generated globally are collected, only 15% are recycled, and the major part is taken to landfills" (Zaman). Some of the waste can be contributed to simple things that can be swapped out for more eco-friendly options. We see this in plastic grocery bags, bubble wrap, and especially plastic water bottles. By buying and using these, we encourage the production. Our dollar is our environmental word and where we spend it correlates with our values. There are very simple ways to become environmentally friendly that are fairly easy.

I find that buying a reusable water bottle and coffee cup, bringing your own bags to the grocery store, or asking for no straw at a restaurant are simple yet effective ways. In addition to doing good for the environment, I'm also saving money. A case of water bottles ranges from $3-5 dollars. Over the course of a year, that can add up to over $150 if bought weekly. By buying a reusable water bottle for under $20, I save about $130 dollars. At my local coffee shop, bringing my own cup I save a dollar off my purchase. Bringing my own grocery bags to the store saves me from paying for paper bags as an eco-friendly option. This doesn't seem like a it saves a lot of money, but it adds up. According to U.S. Environmental Protection Agency, the average person creates 4.40 pounds of trash daily. A solution is to stop this pattern from continuing by switching out habits such as the everyday single use coffee cup. It is important to think about not only the present condition of the Earth, but also having clean Earth for future generations.

Other countries around the world have taken a strong approach to help stop the sale of wasteful packaging. From the Shanghai Daily in China, tea products with an excessive amount packaging were ordered off the shelves and supermarkets that continue to sell these items are fined up to $8,064. By reducing the sales of this product, companies will be forced to redesign packaging to gain back support. This is not to say that the United States has not made changes. According to the National Conference of State Legislators, in November 2016, California became the first state to ban plastic bags and place a fee on their usage. By setting a price on the choice of plastic bags, this encourages the desire of purchasing reusable bags which is a one-time cost compared to paying 10 cents each grocery store trip. The National Conference of State Legislators also provided information about other states have following along such as New York who created a recycling solution by having customers bring back plastic bags to be recycled, Maine who only allows plastic bag usage if there is a recycling bin 20 feet from entrance of store, and North Carolina who posts signs on businesses encouraging reusable bags, but allowing the use of the stores recycled paper bags. There is still a long way to go but progress still has been made.

Thinking about companies' effects on the environment large scale, Amazon is a substantial contributor to the growth of unnecessary waste and packaging. Depending on the size of the item ordered, a great quantity of Amazon packages come in cardboard boxes which can be recycled but along with the order is an unnecessary amount of plastic bubble wrap. This semester, I ordered a book through Amazon that I needed for class because it was cheaper than the bookstore. It came relatively fast and in a cardboard box. After opening, I recycled the box but was left with bubble wrap that protected my paperback book that didn't need extra protection at all. Companies like Amazon need to realize that this is a major problem for small items that are ordered because it is not needed. Forbes Magazine reported that in "Fast Company, about 165 billion packages are shipped in the U.S. each year, with the cardboard used roughly equating to more than 1 billion trees." The reason for an excessive amount of packaging is because "The average box is dropped about 17 times," as reported by Forbes from ANAMA Package and Container Testing owner, Anton Cotaj. Things like my book are not going to matter if they are dropped any amount of times because ultimately, I still get my book. According to the Detroit Free Press, in 2016 Amazon partnered with Goodwill to reuse the boxes for shipping out unwanted goods to an organization called Give Back Box, where these items were sold to "support employment placement, job training, and other community-based services". The company is aware of the trash issue and is finding ways to reuse and recycle these boxes, but I can't help thinking that there is more they could be doing such as providing customers with a size box preference for their orders. Smaller boxes or paper envelopes could help with items that are too small for a regular sized box like my book I ordered.

My grandfather has worked at an office furniture company called Haworth in Holland, Michigan for 30 years. This company is known for being zero-landfill operating. Their *Our Values* page contains a statement saying "We think beyond our business to our communities. We cultivate hope for the future by embracing diversity, protecting our environment, and creating economic value. In our small way, we help make the world a better place for people to work and live" ("At Work"). My grandpa who works in the facility department of Haworth said, "We send our waste to Waste to Energy that burns it to create electricity." He also explained to me that the wood that is unused goes to another company that chips it to make other products out of it. Also, all the scraps of metal, steel, and aluminum go to a recycling plant. The company recycles all carboard and plastic that it creates. "The extra fabric is sent to another company that recycles it into carpeting." All of this zero-waste work can be traced back to Bill Gurn, the company's manager of facilities. Although it can be costly, he has taken the steps to help to global issue of waste though Haworth. He realizes how important it is to help the environment, even in a work setting.

Something I think about in the production of furniture and appliances are second hand or tarnished products. Noble Appliance center located in Hartland, Michigan is a notable example of a different perspective on this issue. They sell kitchen and laundry appliances at a discounted price because of minor scratches or dings in the product. My family recently bought a brand-new stainless-steel double door fridge for $650 dollars when it was originally over $1600. It had a single dent on the left side, a place no one would notice, and we didn't care because the fridge worked just as it should. As humans, we are obsessed with the idea of perfection and it comes at a cost. Perfectly good items get tossed aside because of a single imperfection. Not all damaged goods go to resale companies. Yale Appliances and Lighting has a page on their website titled, "Your Appliance is Damaged Upon Delivery, Now What?". In the help page, it contains a paragraph about suggesting living with a minorly damaged appliance. The example they give is the exact same my family encountered with our fridge. They promote the use of the products even if there is a small scratch because ultimately it will still perform the same. Other companies like Home Depot have a different perspective. Upon searching through their website titled "About Your Online Order", I found a small explanation of if items arrive damaged. This had information about who to call to get a replacement or refund, or what to do if you refuse the product because of its condition. There was nothing to be found about guidelines of what constitutes as damage or alternative options for possibly living with the product. The question then arises, where do these appliances end up? Talking on the phone with multiple Home Depot representatives, I gathered that no one really knows where they go. After being transferred three times because no one could answer my question, I spoke to a representative from GE appliances, who said quote; "As far as I know they might go to a scratch and dent center, but I really don't know . . . that's a good question." It is important to know where our unwanted goods end up because it helps show the environmental effects they have.

We have all heard the phrase, "there is no planet B", and it is true especially when it comes to the environment. Being conscious about our economic decisions impacts not just our wallet, but our world. Creating habits throughout our life can add up to a big change. I started out buying bamboo toothbrushes, but now I have grown to be conscious about where my dollar is spent every day and how it affects my environment. When we take care of the environment, it gives us a sense of accomplishment and fulfillment. We are the people creating the trash so we are the only ones to find solutions for it. Not only are we saving the environment, but we also save money by choosing not to buy bottled water or invest in companies with excess packaging because ultimately, we are also paying for the production of that. For me, it started with a toothbrush, for others, any small step can spark inspiration into the lifestyle of living with less trash.

*Word Count: 1800*

## Works Cited

"About Your Online Order." *The Home Depot,* 2000, www. homedepot.com/c/About_Your_Online_Order. Accessed 28 Feb. 2019.

"At Work, on the Go, at Home. Work Happens Everywhere." *About Us | Haworth,* www.haworth.com/company-info/about-us. Accessed 13 Mar. 2019.

Bird, Jon. "What A Waste: Online Retail's Big Packaging Problem." *Forbes,* 29 Jul. 2018, https://www.forbes.com/sites/jonbird1/2018/07/29/what-a-waste-online-retails-big-packaging-problem/#221887b0371d.

National Conference of State Legislatures. *State Plastic and Paper Bag Legislation,* 2019, www.ncsl.org/research/environment-and-natural-resources/plastic-bag-legislation.aspx. Accessed 20 Mar. 2019.

Pietzsch, Natália, et al. "Benefits, Challenges and Critical Factors of Success for Zero Waste: *A Systematic Literature Review." Waste Management*, vol. 67, 2017, pp. 324–353. *Science Direct,* doi.org/10.1016/j.wasman.2017.05.004.

Robinson, Elissa. "Ship Your Donations to Goodwill in Unwanted Amazon Boxes." *Detroit Free Press,* 28 Dec. 2016, www.freep.com/story/money/business/2016/12/22/amazon-goodwill-charity-donations-ship/95754848/.

Sheinkopf, Steve, *Your Appliance Is Damaged Upon Delivery. Now What?" Home Appliance & Lighting Blog,* 29 Jul. 2017, www. blog.yaleappliance.com/your-appliance-is-damaged-upon-delivery.-now-what.

"Tea Products with Excessive Packaging Ordered Off Shelves." *Shanghai Daily,* 8 Jun. 2013, https://search.proquest.com/ docview/1365786413/fulltext/1E6AD15122A54306PQ/1?acc ountid=39473.

U.S. Environmental Protection Agency. *Wastes-Non-Hazardous Waste-Municipal Waste:Municipal Solid Waste.* 29 Mar. 2016, archive.epa.gov/epawaste/nonhaz/municipal/web/html/.

# LIVING IN TOXICITY

## Kayla Weaver

Kayla Weaver is a Finance and Accounting major from St. Clair, Michigan. She was interested in writing about toxic waste on the St. Clair River in Professor Craig Hulst's class because her "immediate family and friends have developed rare illnesses with undetermined causes," possibly caused by toxic waste. For that reason, Kayla is proud of this essay because it's an issue important to her community and herself, and she enjoyed becoming more knowledgeable about this topic by exploring it through research and writing.

St. Clair County, Michigan encompasses several small towns bordering the west bank of the St. Clair River. During the warmer months, lots of people are out on the water, partaking in water sports, boating, fishing, and more. Some people refuse to go into the water at all, and for good reason. Forty percent of Canada's petrochemical industry is located in Sarnia, the city that is located eight hundred feet across from the county, giving the area the nickname, "Chemical Valley" (Bagelman and Wiebe). With more than sixty petrochemical plants, Chemical Valley's annual combined air release of pollutants is over an astounding 132 million kilograms (MacDonald and Rang 17). The contaminated air has made Chemical Valley infamous for its alarmingly high rates of cancer, autism, fertility problems, and cardiovascular diseases among its population (McGuire). On top of the health concerns that come with living along the St. Clair River, the water is extremely polluted, causing great harm to the river's ecosystem, which directly impacts the economies of the cities surrounding it. If the pollution produced from the plants in Chemical Valley is not restricted further, the troubling implications from the toxicity will continue to worsen until the effects are irreversible.

Communities on both sides of the St. Clair River are familiar with the adverse health effects associated with living in the area, especially the Natives that reside on the Aamjiwnaang First Nation reserve in Sarnia, Canada. The reserve is located less than twenty-five kilometers away from about thirty chemical facilities, giving members of the band the greatest exposure to the toxic pollutants.

---

Several studies have been conducted to determine the consequences of such conditions on their health, all coming to the same conclusion that one living in Chemical Valley has a significantly increased risk of developing a wide range of diseases as a result of chronic exposure to pollutants (Olawoyin).

Elaine MacDonald and Sarah Rang outlined the troubling results from a particular survey conducted in 2005 in their report "Exposing Canada's Chemical Valley." The Aamjiwnaang Environment Committee surveyed members of the reserve regarding their health. Forty percent of the people surveyed required an inhaler for their respiratory issues. Close to thirty percent reported high blood pressure, persistent headaches, breathing troubles, and worsening asthma. Moreover, thirty-nine percent of women experienced a miscarriage or a stillbirth, while the nationwide average for a miscarriage in Canada is twenty percent ("Incidence of Early Loss of Pregnancy" 1483). It was also discovered that there is an imbalanced sex ratio among the reserve, with a notable steady decrease of male births since the early 1990s. The high rates of these health issues have an obvious connection to the reserve's close proximity to chemical plants.

Moving onto the province of Ontario as a whole, Sarnia has a population of around 70,000 people, Windsor has 217,000 and London has 380,000, yet Sarnia still has significantly more hospitalizations than both of those cities. These hospitalizations were majorly for respiratory and cardiovascular diseases, the rates of which are much higher in Sarnia than in nearby cities (MacDonald and Rang 9-10). The only explanation for the high rates of hospitalizations in Sarnia compared to other cities in Ontario is that Sarnia is home to a great number of plants and factories. Clearly, Sarnia is a hotspot for a number of diseases due to constant vulnerability to harmful toxins.

Sarnia is not the only community infamous for its alarmingly high rates of disease in Chemical Valley. On the other side of the river, an investigation was held by the St. Clair County Health Department in 2012 to determine the cause of the Wilms Tumor cluster. Wilms Tumor is an extremely rare cancer of the kidneys that affects young children. Between 1990 and 2009, there was a total of eleven cases in St. Clair County, with seven of the children diagnosed younger than five years of age ("Investigation Summary Report"). "The occurrence of new Wilms tumor cases in St. Clair County was nearly three times higher than expected based on the incidence rate of the rest of Michigan," the Investigation Summary Report stated. The Health Department's investigation was inconclusive in regards to the exact causes of the cluster, yet they still listed potential causes. None of which suggested pollution to be a factor. The Great Lakes Environmental Justice blames politics for the rejection of pollution as a probable cause on the report:

> A local mathematician calculated that to have so many cases of Wilms in such a small community is like winning the lottery twice in a row, consecutively, yet the County Health Department refuses to treat it as anything other than coincidence until proven otherwise. The reasoning behind this is part of a larger problem in the legislation of environmental issues that is becoming increasingly prevalent in the U.S. –a shift in the burden of proof from corporations to citizens ("The Political Landscape of the St. Clair County Cancer Cluster").

Even if the Health Department will not disclose it, there is a connection between the Wilms Tumor cluster in St. Clair County and Chemical Valley, similar to the relation between the increased incidence rates of Hodgkin's Disease and leukemia in Sarnia. MacDonald and Rang found that "Hodgkin's disease amongst males was 80 percent higher than the rest of Ontario and leukemia incidents amongst women between the ages of 25 and 44 was more than double the Ontario rate" (10). The statistics prove what the St. Clair County Health Department lacked in their findings; the correlation between clusters of rare diseases and living in Chemical Valley.

Another attribute that comes with living in this area is odor annoyance. It is caused by airborne pollutants and it is the source of several health complications that affect everyday life for the people residing in Chemical Valley. A journalist from *Vice* visited Sarnia, and wrote about his experience with odor annoyance. "The first thing you notice about Sarnia, Ontario, is the smell: a potent mix of gasoline, melting asphalt, and the occasional trace of rotten egg. Shortly after my arrival I already felt unpleasantly high and dizzy, like I wasn't getting enough air" ("The Chemical Valley"). The symptoms named by the journalist developed from short term exposure only. Those vulnerable to strong odors everyday are susceptible to a range of health issues. Irritation of the eyes, nose, throat and lungs is common, and these can develop into breathing problems. Strong odors can also cause headaches and nausea accompanied by psychosocial modifications such as changes in mood, anxiety, and stress levels ("Odors & Health"). The health issues caused from odor annoyance on top of the increased risk of developing various diseases can be avoided altogether if the pollution in Sarnia is restricted much further.

The consequences of pollution in Chemical Valley extend further than human health complications, there are environmental concerns as well. The St. Clair River is contaminated with an abundance of harmful chemicals, which poses great risk to several bodies of water. The St. Clair River is located at the mouth of Lake Huron, and flows into the Detroit River, which then flows into Lake Erie. Consequently, the pollutants dumped into the St. Clair River have the potential of moving downstream, making cleanup and removal very difficult as crews want to avoid stirring up the chemicals sitting on the riverbed.

The accumulation of lead (Pb) in the St. Clair River is very troubling. In fact, the river has so much lead in it, a lead-resistant bacterial species has evolved as a consequence of long-term exposure to pollutants, according to a journal article by Nichole Bowman et al.:

> In freshwater environments, Pb tends to settle at the bottom of the water where it concentrates and is capable of accumulating in the tissues of aquatic biota. Even at low concentrations, the composition, distribution, and diversity benthic organisms are affected. Thus, removal of toxic heavy metals such as Pb from industrial wastewaters is essential from the standpoint of environmental pollution control.

If we do not find an efficient way to remove lead and keep it out of the St. Clair River, the organisms that live on the bed of the river will continue to suffer the consequences of high concentrations of lead.

Another dangerous chemical found in the river is mercury. In 1970, all fishing in the St. Clair River and Lake St. Clair was temporarily put to a stop due to the mass amounts of mercury discovered in fish. Mercury contamination is still present in the aquatic species in the river, especially in big game fish, averaging around 1.5 parts per million. The Environmental Protection Agency warns against eating fish contaminated with .15 parts per million, meaning that St. Clair fish are contaminated 10 times more than what the EPA deems as dangerous to consume ("Mercury Finally Getting Cleaned Up"). Eating mercury contaminated fish can be very harmful and potentially deadly to humans. In 1956, citizens of Minamata City, Japan began to fall gravely ill due to the same toxic waste disposition processes that Sarnia's plants use, which is dumping everything into the nearest body of water. Approximately 2,200 people became sick and more than 1,000 people died as a result consuming fish that were contaminated with mercury from a factory dumping their toxic waste into the Minamata Bay (Harada 1). This illness, coined Minamata Disease, is likely to come about in Chemical Valley if there is no progress in chemical removal as there is just as much, if not more, mercury in the river today as there was in 1970.

With the profusion of pollution in the river affecting its ecosystem, the cities surrounding the St. Clair River and Lake St. Clair that are largely dependent on fishing will continue to have negative impacts on their economies. Already, there are fewer fish in the river and lake because there are limited habitable spawning areas, which is distressing for the surrounding cities. Mackey states in his report, "the sport fishery on Lake St. Clair is substantial, supporting one of the most valuable recreational fisheries in the world for walleye, yellow perch, smallmouth bass, and muskellunge." Furthermore, thirty-three percent of all fish and forty-eight percent of sport fish caught in the Great Lakes are fished out of Lake St. Clair. The annual value of recreational fishery for Michigan and Ontario combined is more than $30 million. Recreational boating also contributes $249 million every year to both economies (Mackey 8). Pollutants must be removed and kept out of the river or there will be no one boating or fishing because the river will be too toxic.

To conclude, the effects of pollution on public health, aquatic ecosystems, and economies of the cities in Chemical Valley is extremely disturbing and profound. It is a shame that the power of large corporations and politics is put before the well-being of thousands of people. Due to the lack of interest and movement on this issue from the government, more effort must be put into restricting the amount of pollutants the plants can release into the air and dumping hazardous wastes in the river should be outlawed. Alternative measures need to be taken to ensure that the people of Sarnia and St. Clair County are just as likely to get a disease as they would anywhere else. Improvements need to be made now before Chemical Valley turns into a dystopia that is ridden with people wearing face masks every time they step outside with fish floating belly-up in the river, and the lingering regret of "we should have done something sooner."

*Word Count: 1919*

## Works Cited

Bagelman, Jen, and Sarah Marie Wiebe. "Intimacies of Global Toxins: Exposure & Resistance in 'Chemical Valley.'" *Political Geography*, vol. 60, 2017, pp. 76–85, doi:10.1016/j.polgeo.2017.04.007.

Bowman, Nichole, et al. "Lead-Resistant Bacteria from Saint Clair River Sediments and Pb Removal in Aqueous Solutions." *Applied Microbiology and Biotechnology*, vol. 102, no. 5, 2018, pp. 2391–2398, doi:10.1007/s00253-018-8772-4.

"The Chemical Valley." *Vice*, 8 Aug. 2013, www.vice.com/en_us/article/4w7gwn/the-chemical-valley-part-1.

Harada, Masazumi. "Minamata Disease: Methylmercury Poisoning in Japan Caused by Environmental Pollution." *Critical Reviews in Toxicology*, vol. 25, no. 1, 25 Sept. 1995, pp. 1–24, doi:10.3109/10408449509089885.

"Incidence of Early Loss of Pregnancy." *New England Journal of Medicine*, vol. 319, no. 22, 28 July 1988, pp. 1483–1484, doi:10.1056/nejm198812013192214.

"Investigation Summary Report." *St. Clair County Health Department*. July 2012.

MacDonald, Elaine, and Sarah Rang. *Exposing Canada's Chemical Valley*. Ecojustice, 2007.

Mackey, Scudder D. *St. Clair River Ecosystem Summary White Paper and Report*. Mar. 2011.

McGuire, Patrick. "Chemical Valley's Children Have Banned Chemicals in Their Blood." *Vice*, 19 Nov. 2013. www.vice.com/en_us/article/mv5ay4/chemical-valleys-children-have-banned-chemicals-in-their-bloodstreams.

"Mercury Finally Getting Cleaned Up." *Times Herald*, 13 Dec. 2018, www.thetimesherald.com/story/opinion/editorials/2018/12/13/mercury-finally-getting-cleaned/38732993/.

"Odors & Health." *Odors & Health*, New York State Department of Health, 2018. www.health.ny.gov/publications/6500/index.htm.

Olawoyin, Richard. "Adverse Human Health Impacts in the Anthropocene." *Environmental Health Insights*, vol. 12, 16 Nov. 2018, doi:10.1177/1178630218812791.

"The Political Landscape of the St. Clair County Cancer Cluster." *Great Lakes Environmental Justice*, 14 June 2012, greatlakesenvironmentaljustice.wordpress.com/st-clair-county/socio-political/.

"St. Clair River." *Detroit District, U.S. Army Corps of Engineers*, U.S. Army Corps of Engineers, 2019, www.lre.usace.army.mil/Missions/Great-Lakes-Information/Outflows/Discharge-Measurements/St-Clair-River/.

The Department of Writing offers a curriculum that teaches students to construct texts that appeal to different audiences, a critical skill for the 21st century. With the proliferation of online and accelerated communication, the ability to tell a story that engages and persuades an audience is more important than ever. A degree in writing can help students develop these skills.

Writing majors and minors will have opportunities to develop storytelling skills in a wide variety of genres and media. Whether students are interested in connecting storytelling to traditional genres (academic, poetry, magazine, fiction, non-fiction) or to the latest writing technologies (document design software, content management systems), they can select courses that best prepare them for future professional careers.

Through a unique modular curriculum that combines courses in professional, academic, and creative writing, students will learn how to create, shape, design, and share texts. These abilities will allow them to enter the world in a variety of careers such as Web writer, freelancer, document designer, magazine writer, editor, publisher, or technical writer, to name a few. The flexibility and the variety of courses offered lets students shape their educational experience and future professional identity.

Through the BA or BS degree, writing majors develop the skill set to:

- ▶ Write fiction and non-fiction texts.
- ▶ Develop and tailor content to both print and online media.
- ▶ Work with the industry standard writing and design software.
- ▶ Collaborate with other writers, editors, subject matter experts, and designers to prepare content for publication.
- ▶ Develop promotional materials to pitch and sell content.

Christopher Toth, Chair
Professor of Writing
Lake Ontario Hall 326
Department of Writing
616-331-3411
www.gvsu.edu/writing

GRAND VALLEY
STATE UNIVERSITY.